SWC
Spirit World
Communications

Life Goes On

in a parallel world beyond time

by

Oliver R Haines

amazon kdp

My grateful acknowledgements to, in particular:

Marc Pittaway

Robin Clayton

Tim Abbott

Ann Evans (Minister, St Luke's Christian Spiritualist Church, Shrewsbury)

Pam Haines (in spirit)

Gwen Haines (in spirit)

Richard Haines (in spirit)

Bill Haines (in spirit)

Alfred Henry Haines (in spirit)

Fred Hammond (in spirit)

My other supporting blood relatives and in-laws (in spirit)

Alfred Quinn (spirit guide)

Edward Seymour (spirit guide)

Demitheria Gutiérrez (spirit guide).

Book design, layout and preparation by Marc L Pittaway, Advertising Matters Ltd, Solihull, UK

Published by Spirit World Communications, Shrewsbury, UK

ISBN 978-1-7398966-0-7

We are not human beings having a spiritual experience.

We are spiritual beings having a human experience.

Pierre Teilhard de Chardin (French Jesuit theologian and scientist, 1881-1955)

Know that the one you love and who loves you has left you physically but not spiritually. Death has no power to separate those whom love has joined together and made them one in spirit.

Trance communication via foremost British medium Maurice Barbanell (1902-1981)

The day science begins to study non-physical phenomena, it will make more progress in one decade than in all the previous centuries of its existence.

Nikola Tesla (Yugoslav-American electrical engineer and inventor, 1856-1943)

A Love of the Sea

Llandanwg beach in wintertime . . . Snow-covered mountains, with straw-coloured sand-dunes running parallel to that backdrop of white mountains like a band of gold. Opposite are sunbeams diffusing into a grey sea at Mochras. Ever changing.

The castle of Criccieth out to sea – sitting on its rock! Then disappearing as the winter sky drops to the sea like a grey stage curtain – the Lleyn Peninsula still visible on one side, and the snow-peaked mountains on the other. A wintry storm is on its way!

Pam Haines, 29th December 2001

Life Goes On

in a parallel world beyond time

by Oliver R Haines

CONTENTS

Life Goes On

in a parallel world beyond time

by Oliver R Haines

PREFACE

This book is a family project to construct a layman's guide aimed at bringing upliftment, comfort and inspiration to those facing death or suffering bereavement and at raising our general understanding of the spirit world after an individual's physical life has ended on earth. It worked for me and it can work for you too, knowing that for everyone there is far more to come.

My book will answer many of your questions and give you a reassuring insight into the new world beyond earthly experience which we shall all ultimately enter. That world does not sit on a heavenly cloud somewhere up above looking down on us mortals, but surrounds us here and now as a parallel existence on a different vibration.

We can enjoy life much more in the here and now if we do not fear death, the unspeakable. The knowledge that there is a new and far superior life on the horizon – free of suffering, mortality and needs – can make such a big difference to us physically and mentally, taking an immense weight off our shoulders.

Our dominant human ego prevents us from imagining that a human life could be merely an adventure, an excursion, an experience and that spirit life might be the normal, continuing state of existence, and yet that is actually the reality. Furthermore we cannot accept the fact that our brainpower is tiny in comparison with the limitless intellect of spirit.

How to describe the spirit world in comprehensible earthly terms has been a challenge throughout the writing process. I have searched for parallels in our physical existence that readers will understand. In particular, putting into words the unique euphoric feeling of love and happiness in the spirit realm has been one of the hardest tasks, being naturally limited by the scope of our vocabulary and language.

So what is my own background? Having been the youngest member of an ageing family on both my mother's and father's side, I have found myself in the position of being the "last man standing" on the earth plane, so that for me an interest in the world of spirit has become a natural progression.

At the many sittings I have had over seven years with my evidential spiritualist medium and friend Robin Clayton, my family in spirit picks a "spokesperson" or prime communicator for the conversation. On different occasions this may be my wife, mother, father, uncle, mother-in-law, father-in-law or other family members of past generations, who will step forward and speak on behalf of the group which chooses to assemble for the purpose of the dialogue.

By way of corroboration, some 50 other mediums have facilitated conversations with my family, chiefly at public platform demonstrations and sittings around the UK over the years.

Coincidentally, the robin as Britain's iconic garden bird is widely regarded as a messenger from spirit, whilst in the 1990s my mother wrote a book "The Christmas Card Bird" on the subject of the robin, as a bearer both of seasonal greetings and of love to family and friends.

So, when my late wife Pam acts as the "anchor" for communication purposes, the rest of the family will stand back and combine as an energy, by teamwork, to assist the dialogue as necessary.

My family's interpretations and impressions of life in the spirit world, and current images and past memories of human life, can be very varied, and they bring forward older spirits with wider experience and deeper knowledge, that is ancestors and other members of their soul group, to contribute, where this would help our understanding.

Spirits communicate via the mind of the medium, a gifted individual able to read, and communicate telepathically with, the consciousness of a transitioned spirit – or indeed a spirit still within a living body – acting as a channel or conduit for messages similar to a telephone line.

Many of you will recall an unexplained experience caused by spirit activity in the past which made you stop and think at the time, and, if you are eager to know more, you will be seeking answers to this in my book.

Then, in common with everyone else, you are bound to have lost one or more

From left to right, Oliver Haines and Robin Clayton carl@capewell.co.uk

family members or friends dear to you at some point in your life. We carry such grief around with us and learn to live with the burden. However if, vitally, you can keep an open mind as to what actually happens to those loved ones in their continuing life, you will be fascinated to read what I have researched and written, developing your own understanding as I have been thrilled to do myself.

Afterlife research frequently converges with related fields of study such as history, philosophy, theology, physics, psychology, sociology and the arts, not to mention with life in general. As a result, the voyage of discovery we embark on together in this book has deep roots, as you will recognise, in our existing knowledge, which we can now expand by working beyond the narrow boundaries of accepted science.

Chapter 1

OUR CULTURAL BACKGROUND TO THE SPIRIT WORLD

Introduction & historical context

What awaits us beyond this physical life? A belief in the afterlife, or life after death, has been part of faiths, religions and tribal societies around the world dating back to the earliest civilisations on our planet. Many belief systems hold that the nature of this continued existence is determined directly by the actions of the individual in his or her earthly life. To this end, a life review or report would occur immediately after death.

Added to ideas about the afterlife, we have the notion, found in many ancient cultures, of reincarnation or rebirth, the philosophical or religious concept that a living being can choose to start a new life in a different physical body or form after each biological death.

In more recent times we have the theological writings and Bible interpretations of the influential Swedish philosopher and scholar Emanuel Swedenborg discussing the realm of spirits. Based upon what he described as revelations through dreams and visions, he was convinced that the Bible describes a human's transformation from a materialistic to a spiritual being, which he calls rebirth or regeneration.

He maintained that the creation story was an allegory of man's rebirth or

Emanuel Swedenborg (1688-1772): a portrait painted by Per Krafft the Elder in about 1766, courtesy of the National Museum, Stockholm

regeneration in six steps represented by the six days of creation. Swedenborg was also convinced of the existence of spirit life on other planets in the universe. His ideas may have been controversial and fiercely debated at the time, but at least he was accorded respect, and achieved a far-reaching and long-lasting influence, based upon the elevated status he was fortunate to have in Swedish society at the time.

Pioneers of modern spiritualism

In Great Britain the English poet, writer and Egyptologist Gerald Massey (1828-1907) is credited as a pioneer of modern spiritualism in his country. He challenged the historical misinterpretation of God's mysteries as described in the Bible, "adopted in ignorance and reissued as real truths by humankind" despite them being no more than inspirational allegories and parables told and retold down the ages. Those misinterpreted stories evidently ranged from the Garden of Eden and the Serpent to the Burning Bush on Mount Horeb, and from God's destruction of Sodom and Gomorrah to Noah's Ark and the Great Flood onwards.

In 1852 an American Mrs Maria Hayden gave the first public demonstration in England of mediumship, and the following year the nation's first Spiritualist Church was opened at Keighley, West Yorkshire.

In 1871 the formidable early English medium Emma Hardinge Britten was the architect of the seven principles of spiritualism as a religion, which we talk about later on.

Emma published her seven religious principles subsequently in the "Two Worlds" spiritualist magazine which she went on to launch in 1887. This remained the principal news organ for spiritualism in Britain until another medium Maurice Barbanell established the "Psychic News" 45 years later in 1932 along with campaigning Fleet Street journalist Hannen Swaffer and Swaffer's accountant Jack Rubens. I say more about Barbanell in the context of trance mediumship in Chapter 8.

From 1906 the editor of "Two Worlds", the literary author James Johnson Morse (1848-1919) made his name as a pioneering trance medium, giving weekly demonstrations and remaining active within the spiritualist movement in England for more than half-a-century.

Another interesting personality was Robert James Lees (1849-1931). Born in Hinckley, Leicestershire, he was a British spiritualist, medium and writer of the late

www.ehbritten.org

The medium Emma Hardinge Britten (1823-1899). Amongst the many milestones in her life, she gave the funeral oration for Abraham Lincoln on Sunday 16th April 1865 before 3,000 people at New York City's iconic Cooper Institute. That was where Lincoln had delivered an historic address against slavery in 1860 before taking over as the 16th US President the following year.

Victorian era and early 20th century. Following the death of Prince Albert in 1861, it is said that the 13-year-old Lees lived for a period in Buckingham Palace so that Victoria could talk to her beloved Albert through him.

Nowadays Lees is best known for claims that psychically he knew the identity of serial killer Jack the Ripper, held responsible for the unsolved London Whitechapel murders of women in 1888. Yet, in October of that year, both the City of London Police and Scotland Yard stubbornly disregarded the advice Lees offered and turned him away.

The trailblazing work of Victor Hugo & Allan Kardec

France was a country where incipient spiritualism typically had to battle against both church and state. During his political and religious exile in the Channel Islands from 1852 to 1870, the great French novelist, dramatist and latterly statesman Victor Hugo, author of The Hunchback of Notre Dame and Les Misérables, became an ambassador for spiritualism.

Robert James Lees

Allan Kardec

He used new mediumistic sciences such as table turning to communicate with those who had passed away. His initial contact was with his daughter Léopoldine, who had drowned at 19 with her new husband Charles and unborn child in a boating tragedy on the Seine in 1843, although Hugo was inspired to then go on and communicate with the spirits of some famous figures from down the ages.

Social justice for the impoverished working class was never far from Victor Hugo's thoughts. He had requested a very quiet, pauper's funeral for himself. And yet, after his death at 83 from pneumonia in 1885, more than two million people attended the procession for his state funeral in Paris, winding its way for hours from the Arc de Triomphe to the Panthéon, where he was interred.

Meanwhile, born into a Catholic barrister's family in Lyon, the educator and author Hippolyte Léon Denizard Rivail (1804-1869), better known under his pen name of Allan Kardec, was the father of modern spiritualist, or more exactly spiritist, thought in France and other countries and accordingly a strong opponent of materialism. He also founded and edited a magazine, "La Revue Spirite", building upon his best-known work "Le Livre des Esprits" ("The Spirits' Book"), published in 1857 in the first of 20 editions.

Structured as a series of over 1000 questions and answers inspired by the spirit world regarding the soul, the afterlife, reincarnation and the laws of God and of nature, this book succeeded in winning over the Emperor Napoleon III, who discussed it with Rivail in meetings they had at the Tuileries Palace in Paris. Nevertheless Rivail's concept of a God endowed with supreme intelligence and power, directing human affairs from on high having first created the universe, had to be appropriate and acceptable to the times and society in which he lived.

Nowadays spiritism, the branch of spiritualism Rivail developed emphasising reincarnation, has many adherents in Anglo-Saxon and Latin American countries and Vietnam. However it is by far the strongest in Brazil, where it has between 20 and 40 million followers and Rivail has featured several times as Allan Kardec on the nation's postage stamps.

German philosophers & thinkers focus on the afterlife

From 1866 onwards, Kardec's writings were also translated into German. Germany has always been a country rich in philosophers, thinkers and researchers and yet is devoid of spiritualist churches. Such churches were banned by the post-War German Federal government as its misguided reaction to the occultism and astrological hokum propagated by Nazi leaders such as Himmler and Rosenberg.

In that country, awareness of the spirit of man as a separate consciousness may be traced back to their renowned philosophers of the 1700s such as Leibniz, Kant and Lessing.

Late in the next century, Baron Carl du Prel of Munich (1839-99), a follower of both Immanuel Kant and Charles Darwin, stood out with his book "The Philosophy of Mysticism", dealing with altered states of consciousness, the psychology of dreams, trance and hypnotic sleep.

Du Prel conducted numerous experiments on hypnotism before moving on to the newly emerging fields of spiritualism and psychical research. Even Sigmund Freud was to cite du Prel's conclusions as being valuable for his master work "The Interpretation of Dreams".

Echoing Kant, who held that the existence of God and the afterlife need to be postulated since they serve as powerful moral regulators, du Prel commented in 1888 that a belief in survival was a necessary condition for altruistic motivation: "It could be demonstrated easily that all social diseases are associated, at their deepest roots, with a generation's view of death. In order to be good, which may be an inbred trait, the belief in immortality might be dispensable, but it is

Baron Carl du Prel

http://kardec.de/announcement/du-prel

Baron Albert von Schrenck-Notzing

indispensable in order to become better."

Another Baron from Munich, Albert von Schrenck-Notzing (1862-1929), was a prominent German psychic investigator and author. Over four decades of study, there was no prominent medium around at the time in Europe with whom he had not conducted experiments. Schrenk-Notzing supervised these under the most rigorous conditions, to explore the physical phenomena which particularly interested him such as materialisations, psychokinesis, telekinesis and ectoplasm.

Development of spiritualism in the USA

From the Russian Empire of the 19th century came a number of original thinkers who, as elsewhere, had to battle against powerful vested interests to get themselves heard. These individuals included the psychic researcher Alexander Aksakoff (1832-1903) and the widely travelled medium – and founder of a pantheistic religious philosophy called theosophy – Helena Blavatsky (1831-1891).

Blavatsky was instrumental in bringing the ancient spiritual wisdom of the East to the modern West, where it was virtually unknown. The first Russian woman to be naturalised as an American citizen, she established the Theosophical Society in New York City in 1875. It incorporated aspects of Buddhism and Brahmanism, especially the belief in reincarnation and spiritual evolution.

Helena Blavatsky in 1877

Andrew Jackson Davis (1826-1910) of Orange County, south-eastern New York State, was another trailblazer in the development of modern spiritualism on the other side of the Atlantic.

Formal education in spiritualist practice emerged there in the 1920s, within organisations like the William T Stead Memorial Center of Chicago, Illinois and the Morris Pratt Institute. Located nowadays in Milwaukee, Wisconsin, the latter is a teaching centre for the National Spiritualist Association of Churches (NSAC), a body founded at a three-day convention in Chicago in 1893.

Another NSAC centre for spiritualist studies is in the village of Lily Dale, south-western New York State. Lily Dale is home to the USA's oldest continuously operating spiritualist community, dating back to 1879 and accommodating more than 50 male and female registered mediums. Each year 20 to 30 thousand visitors come to this village for mediumship and spiritual healing demonstrations, readings, lectures, classes and workshops.

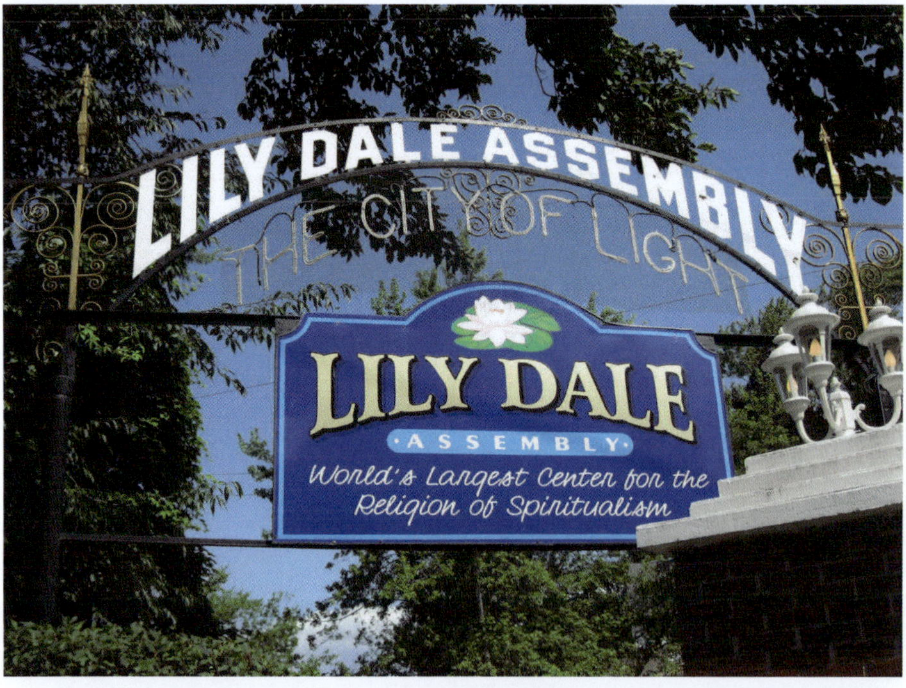

Entrance to the hamlet of Lily Dale in New York State, which became known as the Lily Dale Assembly in 1906. From its inception the purpose of this gated community has been to further the general understanding and appreciation of spiritualism.

More broadly, when you consider that some 75 to 85 million people died in the course of two World Wars, and over 50 million in the global Spanish Flu pandemic of 1918-19, internationally hundreds of thousands of the bereaved have historically turned to, and found comfort through, genuine mediums.

Sir Arthur Conan Doyle

Among other personalities, at the summit of his literary fame with the Sherlock Holmes novels, Sir Arthur Conan Doyle decided to abandon writing fiction and devote himself almost entirely to a study of the paranormal. Conan Doyle was convinced that intelligence could exist apart from the body, and that the dead could communicate with the living.

His two-volume collection of essays chronicling numerous mediumistic experiments, experiences and psychic investigations titled "The History of Spiritualism", published in 1926 by Cassell in London, was one of over 20 authoritative books and pamphlets that he wrote on the subject between the end of World War 1 and his own passing in 1930. He was also made President of the International Spiritualist Federation (ISF), founded in 1923 at Liège, Belgium, in the aftermath of the World War.

Sir Arthur Conan Doyle, 1859-1930
Portrait by an unknown artist, courtesy of Portsmouth Museums & Visitor Services

Society for Psychical Research, London

Like Conan Doyle, Lord Arthur Balfour, British Prime Minister from 1902 to 1905 and Foreign Secretary 1916 to 1919, was, prior to assuming those responsibilities, an active member of the Society for Psychical Research (SPR), formed in London in February 1882: he became its President too. The SPR spearheaded research into all forms of mediumship to expose con artists and magicians' tricks and prove who was genuine. Its vast archive of historical investigations has been housed since 1989 in the Cambridge University Library.

A principal founder of the SPR was the highly respected scientist and metallurgist Sir William Fletcher Barrett (1844-1925), who was involved in psychical research for 50 years. He was a Fellow of the Royal Society (FRS), the Philosophical Society and the Royal Society of Literature and member of the Institute of Electrical Engineers, as well as holding the Chair of Physics at the Royal College of Science in Dublin for 37 years up to retirement.

The British physicist and mathematician Sir Oliver Lodge (1851-1940) was the first Professor of Physics at the University of Liverpool, holding the post from

Physics professors Sir William Fletcher Barrett (left) and Sir Oliver Lodge (right) were leading British scientists of their age who were also Presidents of the Society for Psychical Research at the beginning of the 1900s

1881 to 1900. As a leading scientist of his age, he is remembered mainly for his development of key patents for wireless technology and electromagnetism. He served as President of the SPR from 1901 to 1903 and again in 1932.

After his son, Raymond, was killed in World War 1 in 1915, he visited several mediums and wrote about the experience in a number of books, including the best-selling ***Raymond or Life and Death*** (1916). That book documented the sittings which he and his wife Mary had attended with a celebrated British trance medium, Gladys Osborne Leonard. Oliver Lodge was a friend of Arthur Conan Doyle.

Two founder members of the SPR, Professor Frederic Myers and Dr Richard Hodgson, also feature in our discussion of automatic spirit writing (psychography) in Chapter 8.

More recently, Battle of Britain icon Air Chief Marshal Lord Hugh Dowding was, along with his wife Muriel, also a committed spiritualist and theosophist, and his books published after the end of the War collectively support the idea of the survival of the spirit after physical death.

Nevertheless, in this present book I am not talking about ideas and beliefs from the past, but rather facts based on current interviews with spirits, in which they were asked directly about their experiences in the afterlife.

Religious intolerance & persecution

As for my own background, I have emerged from a strict Church-of-England upbringing to speak for the world of spirit, which is an evidence-based reality or "way of life" as distinct from merely a set of beliefs, an ideology or a religion. Knowing things is very different from simply believing in them.

My earliest religious education at a private primary school in Solihull, Warwickshire (now West Midlands) in the 1950s now seems so incredibly distorted and intolerant.

In that setting Christianity was hailed as consistently reflecting virtue and perfection down the ages, whilst major, non-Christian, faiths ranging from Buddhism, Hinduism and Islam to the more localised Shinto, Sikhism and Taoism were denounced by schoolmasters – from platform and pulpit alike – as the heathenistic spawn of the devil, from which people needed to be saved at all cost.

In reality there are an estimated 4200 different religions around the globe. Among the small number of what may be called world religions, Christianity and Islam certainly predominate, each with more than one billion adherents.

The irony is that, for centuries right into the 1800s, world history has demonstrated the extreme inhumanity and brutal torture exerted at all levels by Roman Catholics and Protestants alike of the Christian faith upon heretics accused of disagreeing with them. Arguably all religions should be about showing tolerance, love and compassion towards fellow human beings.

The barbaric massacres over two centuries in the Holy Land by Christian Crusaders from Europe are well documented in our history books. But Crusades were also widely employed elsewhere to eliminate those whom the Pope regarded as heretics. One of the first genocides in history was the Albigensian Crusade of 1209 to 1229, when Pope Innocent III had up to a million Cathars wiped out in the Languedoc region of south-eastern France.

The conduct of the Spanish Inquisition

250 years later, another papal bull or edict, issued this time by Sixtus IV in 1478, established the Spanish Inquisition, which continued in Spain and its colonies for over 350 years until its official abolition by the Spanish queen regent in 1834.

The first Inquisitor General of Spain, the notorious Castilian Dominican friar Torquemada, had thousands of allegedly heretic Jews and Muslims burned alive over a 15-year reign of terror, with the full support of three successive Popes.

People were often tortured to force religious conversions. They also faced torture when accused of heresy against the Catholic Church. Indeed, in Spain as elsewhere, instruments of torture were usually blessed by a priest before use.

Accordingly countless unfortunates were tortured or burned at the stake during the Spanish Inquisition on the pretext of religious heresy or conversion, although the Inquisitors (like the French noblemen leading the Crusade against the Cathars) were often motivated by more earthly concerns – they wanted to take over the estates and wealth of their victims.

The Magdalene laundries in Ireland

Across the island of Ireland, orders of nuns, in collusion with the government of the day, ran the infamous Magdalene laundries and mother-and-baby homes for so-called "fallen women", unmarried mothers and social outcasts. Women who had a child out of wedlock were branded as criminals subject to "the wrath of God", the divine response from the Old Testament to human sin and disobedience.

Over a 200-year period from the 18th to the second half of the 20th century, tens of thousands of young females were enslaved in Magdalene institutions in Ireland, including over 11,000 since Irish independence in 1922. The inhuman treatment of these desperate women and their unwanted children by cruel and sadistic sisters, allegedly meting out due punishment "in the name of God", has only in recent years been exposed to public scrutiny.

Perverse beliefs which underpin mass killings

On the recurring theme of anti-Semitism, the Reichskonkordat signed in Rome with the Vatican in July 1933 gave Hitler and the Nazis a free hand to proceed later with the Holocaust, unchallenged by the Catholic Church.

The Concordat granted freedom of practice to the Roman Catholic Church, which in return agreed to separate religion from politics. For most of the Holocaust the then Pope Pius XII maintained a public front of indifference and remained silent whilst Jews – regarded as subhuman according to perverted Nazi racial ideology – were being deported across the European Continent for mass gassing. Consistently besieged with pleas for help on behalf of the Jews, Pius XII refused them on the grounds of neutrality, instead making vague statements condemning injustices in general.

There is strong evidence from Jewish organisations that, even after World War 2 was over, more than a few senior Nazi criminals and collaborators escaped prosecution by recourse to so-called "ratlines" operated via a network of sympathetic Vatican contacts and foreign politicians. False papers were quickly provided for travel, as was temporary sanctuary at monasteries. These routes went through Spain and Italy to safe havens in Latin America where identities could be permanently changed.

Subversion of honest faith into cults

Human beings like to fill a psychological void in their lives with a belief system – such as a religion conducted in bricks-and-mortar churches – and yet the misdirection of that honest Christian faith into cults has been an issue throughout history.

November 18th 1978 saw the notorious Jonestown massacre in north-western Guyana, where more than 900 people committed suicide simultaneously with cyanide and tranquillisers at a settlement run by Christian cult leader, the messianic Jim Jones.

Jones had used the manipulative psychological technique of gaslighting (derived from George Cukor's 1944 thriller movie Gaslight), applying it slowly and progressively so that the victims did not realise how much they had been brainwashed. Before the four coordinated attacks on US soil by the al-Qaeda terrorist organisation on September 11th 2001, Jonestown was the largest single incident of intentional civilian death in American history.

In 2000 Uganda suffered a massacre by a millennium doomsday cult of lapsed Catholics which killed over 700 followers locked inside a burning Christian church at Kanungu. The perpetrators, the cult leaders, left the scene and have never been traced.

Meanwhile, in Muslim-majority countries who practise Sharia religious law, men and women who wish to leave Islam, converting to another faith or totally disengaging from religion, can still now, in the 21st century, be punished for that by public execution.

Kindness breeds more kindness

So, by way of an aside, this is my personal view – based upon historical events – of the evil deeds perpetrated "in the name of" religions and ideologies, thereby masking any good that they may do, and it may or may not correspond with your own opinion as a reader.

But I might add that, here and now, hardly a week goes by without the exposure of some cardinal, minister, vicar or priest for misusing his authority and criminally abusing young people over whom he has power. To protect the reputation of the Church, reports of child sex abuse have often been ignored or suppressed by Church leaders.

Certainly people tend always to be far more concerned in their lives with tomorrow not yesterday, and to overlook the errors and horrors of the past simply because they lie in the past. In an ideal world there would be no extreme religious intolerance, but, as we all know, it is still very much alive today and sadly will remain so in the future.

Adherence to any earthly religion, cult or ideology is a matter of personal perspective. On the downside, they can so easily "make you a prisoner of your own

Compassion in action. So reminding us of the worldwide hit ballad by The Hollies in 1969 "He Ain't Heavy, He's My Brother", Good Samaritan Patrick Hutchinson carries an injured far-right demonstrator to safety during a Black Lives Matter protest that turned violent by the Southbank Centre in central London on 13th June 2020.

mind". To retain any moral authority, their value in spiritual terms can only lie in how far they may bring out the best in people and encourage them to be selfless, honest and peaceful, to love and help others, to support deserving charities and to share fundamental resources around fairly.

Compassion, neighbourliness and self-sacrifice breed more of the same, just as cruelty and barbarity engender deep bitterness and possibly retaliation in kind, sometimes for generations to come.

Positive human interaction in helping and providing for less fortunate people for purely altruistic reasons can spread as a practice across society, being comparable to the ripples radiating out from a pebble dropped in a pond. Indeed, with the twin impacts of a rising and ageing population, many services in society can only be maintained nowadays by an increasing army of volunteers and charities, since central and regional governments and local councils are regularly short of money.

So what is the position in the 21st century?

In the 21st century, 98% of the people who have ever existed have passed, so that just 2% are currently living out lives on the earth plane (7.5 billion), including around 1.4 billion in both China and India, the world's most populous nations. Hence that overwhelming proportion of 98% from past millennia are now in the spirit realms, where there is infinite space, as hard as that is for us to comprehend.

However, most of those who have physically passed and live on in the spirit world will in fact have been reincarnated and have returned to the earth plane, possibly several times. Hence statistical totals are misleading.

Beyond the bounds of classical physics

The lives that spirit entities live are beyond the bounds of classical physics – or the current understanding of even our most advanced scientists. Science is lagging far behind and has not yet reached the point where it can prove the existence and reality of the spirit world.

There are notable exceptions among scientists in which open-minded science prevails over dogma. For the Italian quantum physics theoretician and science populariser Professor Carlo Rovelli, science is a continuous process of exploring possible new views of the world. Accordingly science, whilst acknowledging the immense legacy of historical knowledge, must also be prepared to challenge its validity. Nothing should be sacrosanct.

To those like Rovelli, the foundation of science is not certainty, but the very opposite, an inherent uncertainty about our own knowledge, an acute awareness of the extent of our own ignorance.

Registering changes in electromagnetic energy

Nevertheless 21st century scientists will at least use EEG (electroencephalography) headsets to physically measure the changes in the brainwaves of mediums as they communicate with spirits.

But beyond this, without going too far into the complex science of electromagnetism with its magnetic flux densities measured in Gauss or Tesla, a handheld Gaussmeter detector, a type of magnetometer, can register the small fluctuations in ambient electromagnetic fields potentially caused by spirit activity.

There again, the concept of electronic voice phenomena (EVP) – spirit voices which may be interposed in electronic recordings or radio broadcasts as anomalous speech or white noise – works on the basis of spirit energy as an electromagnetic energy. Certainly thousands of EVP recordings intriguing to scientists have been logged and archived over the years.

Added to this, we have the technique of Kirlian photography to demonstrate changes in the electromagnetic energy field or aura emanating from all living things, pictured in Chapter 12.

The whole branch of study described above coincides with British physics professor Sir Oliver Lodge's ground-breaking research into electromagnetism in the early 1900s. As mentioned in Chapter 1, at that time he was also President of the Society for Psychical Research in London.

The eternal "Now" in a world without time

It must be said that even the leading scientific minds of the 21st century, too often assigned to their projects by business sponsors, are not free agents able to research how time and consciousness work. The bulk of modern scientific experiments are dictated either by current government strategy or by commercial profit. The notions of pure science – studied for its own sake without regard to its practical applications and quantifiable benefits to life – and of the enquiring mind aching to satisfy its natural curiosity have arguably gone out of fashion or fallen by the wayside.

Our physical world is forever governed by time

If time did not exist, you would be looking at the past, present and future now, in real time: they would all play out at the same time. There would be an eternal "Now". And so it is for beings in the spirit world, who never age and therefore find times and dates irrelevant.

In defence of theoretical physics, you could argue that an illustration of the space-time continuum given in Einstein's Theory of General Relativity, a way of proving that time is always relative to the observer, is the ability which he describes to see a whole movie instantly before your eyes and without time lapse. Einstein famously wrote: "The distinction between the past, present and future is only a stubbornly persistent illusion."

In our linear world, the passage of time means everything. Yet do we regard time as intrinsically linear because that is only what our limited brain capacity is capable of comprehending? We live by time, date, night-and-day, and day-of-the-week, whereas spirit beings have got none of that. They live by a myriad of detailed recollections and experiences that remain in the memory banks of their persona as if they had all happened yesterday.

For instance, they can picture every detail of their family home as it was during their lifetime (showing it thus to an evidential medium). And other family spirits in their vicinity could relive that same experience from history alongside them, rather like watching a film together.

Our concept of "time" is replaced by "experience"

To underline the fact that there is no such thing as "time" in their world, a century on earth can be little more than a second in eternity. "Time" as we know it here is replaced by "experience" and exists only with regard to the spirit's volition to move forward. And so we have "previous" or "past" lives.

To help us to understand this, my family members in spirit have suggested certain analogies from our physical world to show us how irrelevant or unrelated time can be in comparison to your experience, the bigger picture of what you do in your life.

These parallels include the importance of the mileage history of a vehicle (i.e. its experience) in comparison to its life or time span – because it can be parked for a long period on a drive or in a garage doing nothing. Then birds, bees and tortoises may have an identical number of heartbeats over their lives, and yet tortoises, as a species with a slower body clock, enjoy a far longer life experience. Or the fitness fanatic who spends hours in the gym may lead an otherwise idle existence.

Moreover, as concentrated balls of pure energy, spirits can move about instantaneously, at the speed of thought. They see and feel each other as energy. They have no physical limits as regards space and distance and can literally be "here, there and everywhere" in a fraction of a second.

Professor Stephen Hawking (1942-2018), the theoretical physicist, cosmologist, author and former Director of Research at the Centre for Theoretical Cosmology in the University of Cambridge, explained the likes of the Big Bang and black holes in works including his most famous one "A Brief History of Time". And yet all that he wrote is related to time and space as we either know or can imagine it.

Chapter 2

SPIRITS & THEIR WORLD

Same spirit energies have lived on since the dawn of time

A spirit comprising pure energy resides in every life form, every species, on earth. A network of energy flows through all living things – human, animal, tree and plant life alike, as if they are all interconnected and part of a single whole – and one of the surest axioms of science is that energy is indestructible.

Getty Images

A representation of a spirit form characterised by intense luminosity, fast vibration and light energy. The faster the vibrations of the spirit body, the brighter the aura and the lighter the energy. In contrast, our physical world is limited by its slow vibrations and dense energy. As raw, indestructible energy, all spirit beings can move at the speed of thought and pass through solid walls.

In reality, their gender and ethnicity would come across as non-specific, since each spirit on the spirit plane is a composite consciousness of all its previous lives, male or female, within any nation. Nonetheless the personality and appearance which are generally going to be the most prominent and identifiable are those from the spirit's last physical life, which it can successfully project to people with the gift of mediumistic abilities.

Albert Einstein's hypothesis is that no new energies are ever created, but that existing ones merely evolve and change form. To quote his words: "Energy cannot be created or destroyed, it can only be changed from one form to another."

Since the spirit world is not a world of matter but of energy, mind and thought, the energy of spirits is eternal and cannot decay or die. The spirit energy of every one of us has been present since the beginning of time, as hard as that is for us to take on board in earthly terms. There is neither beginning nor end, since spirits are ageless and live forever.

As the human form has evolved physically from early man, so spirits have gone through different stages of evolution, accumulating ever more experience and knowledge over the millennia.

It is also true that the hugely expanded global population now, as compared with thousands of years ago, gives spirits far more opportunities to embrace a physical human life.

If the entire human race were to be wiped out by some man-made, epidemiological or natural disaster, then the greater spirit world would not be harmed in any way. It would continue to exist throughout the interdependent, organic unity of the universe, and a spirit entity should, in theory at least, be able to communicate by thought with another spirit within any life form on literally any planet out there.

The impossibility of reincarnation in humans if they were all to be annihilated would merely slow down the advancement of spiritual energy. Unlike us, the spirit dimension has no needs and does not actually need the earth. That is not to say that the spirit world is not deeply concerned about the future survival of life on earth, because it is, all the time.

Spirits only ever encounter death when they inhabit a mortal human or animal form that inevitably moves on. And as more and more people return to the spirit world, they make the energy there ever stronger.

Perceiving the world by vibrational energy

Different to physical beings like us, spirit entities operate fundamentally on their chosen levels of vibration. The higher the vibration to which spirits can ascend, the more remote they are from the rough physicality of our world.

Possessing neither a body nor our five senses, they perceive everything in the universe by the vibrational energy radiating from it.

Around them are the bright and vivid colours of other energy forms. To them any human, animal, plant, leaf or tree in the physical world is a glowing energy form, with nothing of the physical shape, solidity and characteristics that we would recognise.

Spirits can choose to communicate and interact with us as individuals by temporarily lowering their vibration to our very basic, low level and experiencing our physical reality alongside us. Within that experience, to them nothing is solid, so that they can pass effortlessly through our walls and closed doors when they accompany us.

When you think about it, vibrational energy is emitted by all living creatures as well as by inanimate objects, places, sounds and colours through to physical movements, thoughts, memories and emotions. I show examples later in the book – such as the vibrational frequencies of different colours within visible light (Chapter 3) and Kirlian photography of the luminous electromagnetic aura which exists around all living things (Chapter 12).

Communicating by telepathic thought

Using intellectual energy rather than any physical brain, spirits communicate with one another by telepathic thought and not speech. When one spirit thinks of another, the other will come close. And, much like a radio signal transmitted through the ether or an email message flashing around the world, thoughts can travel to India and back in a second.

Accordingly there is no talking and furthermore no need for names as identification. Indeed, spirits have very little need for anything, whereas as physical human beings we have needs for almost everything.

To reiterate the point above, spirits use none of our five senses. And nor do they exhibit our human emotions except for a highly elevated form of love. Nevertheless they do retain detailed memories of those five senses – and of their feelings and emotions – from the experiences of their past mortal life and are able to project them to other spirits as well as to evidential mediums.

The consciousness, intellect & personality live on

The reality of the spirit world is what the individual mind makes it – that reality is thought, because the physical brain and body are decomposing in the coffin. The indestructible consciousness, intellect and energy field of each spirit live on with his or her personality and individual thoughts, opinions and memories.

A good way of looking at it is that our mind or "subconsciousness" becomes a full "consciousness" when we return to the spirit world. On our transition, that consciousness takes over the controlling role of the now dead brain. That is how the experienced spirit guide Edward Seymour described it to me when he came through in a trance sitting at Stafford, UK, on February 8th 2022.

Reflecting scientists' findings that I discuss in Chapters 3 and 4, the physical brain functions as only a transmitter of consciousness, similar to a radio, and not its originator.

The consciousness remains as strong in the spirit world as it ever was on the physical plane. If it can find any way to communicate a message, it will often convey the regrets of the person for their past action or omission, or express displeasure or a warning about something going on currently among their family or friends.

The surviving consciousness can display a passionate determination to set the historical record straight, most notably when, for example, a miscarriage of justice or other unfairness may have had devastating consequences for the person's life.

At 8am on Tuesday 9th February 1961, 21-year-old George Riley was the last person to be hanged at the Dana prison behind Shrewsbury's main railway station. This was carried out for his alleged murder of a 62-year-old local woman, despite the weak case for the prosecution at Stafford Assizes lacking any forensic evidence or witnesses.

An experienced medium, Mrs Shirley Ford of Bridgnorth, recently did a guided tour of the former prison and received communication in her head from George languishing in the condemned cell. He pleaded tearfully that he was wholly innocent and named a male relative of his who he claimed had actually committed the murder for which George was hanged.

Conveying pictures telepathically

Thoughts passed on within the spirit world are of concepts and experiences devoid of all linguistic differences – to communicate in that world, there is absolutely no need for English, French, Russian, Arabic, Urdu, Swahili, Mandarin Chinese and so forth.

A spirit wishing to communicate "apple" to a spirit on the other side of the world does not need to translate it, but only to convey the picture of an apple by thought, telepathically as pure intellectual energy. Such mind pictures also play a key role in evidential mediumship, where equally spirit is communicating with spirit.

Echoing this, thought experiments have been a classic tool used by many great thinkers stretching back to the ancient Greeks and Romans, enabling us to explore often impossible situations and predict their implications and outcomes.

The German-born theoretical physicist Albert Einstein (1879-1955), pictured here after receiving the Nobel Prize for Physics in 1921

The thought experiments behind Einstein's Theory

Visual thought experiments ("Gedankenexperimente") were a key technique employed by theoretical physicist Albert Einstein to grapple with subjects such as energy, space and time, which also happen to lie at the very core of the spirit world.

And in a similar way to how spirits will use mind pictures to communicate information to us (demonstrated in Chapter 8), he liked to think in pictures. They allowed him to elucidate the mathematics of the space-time continuum in his Theory of General Relativity. The incidence of matter gets space and time to curve, whilst space and time get matter to move.

Via his powerful visual images, Einstein demonstrated that the speed of light is constant and yet the flow of time varies for different people. Time and space are always relative to the observer. Moreover gravity and acceleration are the same thing.

In essence Einstein used pure thought in developing his cosmic theories which changed the face of science, conceptualising complex scientific ideas by imagining real-life scenarios.

Human characteristics no longer the differentiator

With no differentiation in the spirit world as regards language or nationality, no differences exist there either in gender, age, race, skin colour, appearance, social status and sexual orientation. These are things perceived to be so important to our human identity and sadly often giving rise to discrimination, persecution and worse in the physical world.

Simply put, the distinction between one spirit and another is only one of knowledge and expertise gained from individual experience. A sufferer on earth from, for example, personality dysfunction, Down's syndrome, learning disability or one of the acute neurodegenerative diseases will be as fluent, articulate and intelligent as anyone else in the spirit world. The body's ills and needs are left entirely behind.

Travelling here, there & everywhere

To recreate purely physical activities from memories, understandably spirits must have experienced them in their human life, otherwise they cannot do so. However, this is quite different to their significant ability to travel "here, there and everywhere" as a spiritual, not physical, experience in real time. They can traverse the globe in a moment of thought and are constantly discovering fascinating new things.

Even if they had never visited that country during their earthly existence, spirits can think about being in Mexico and instantly be there, experiencing that environment from a spirit point-of-view by combining energies with other spirits in Mexico.

For example, my mother Gwen, with her naturally enquiring mind, had always enjoyed exploring the physical world and recording what she discovered on her travels. Places of particular interest to her which she is now visiting as a spirit, and yet was never able to visit in human form, include: New Delhi, Jubail (Saudi Arabia) and the Pyramids, as well as parts of Africa, Central and South America, Australia, mainland China, Indonesia and Sri Lanka.

Amongst widespread new experiences, she has witnessed the eruption of the Taal volcano in the Philippines and the practice of cannibalism in northern China. She has also been researching the impact of the Indian strain of the Covid-19 virus on New Delhi and the history of the Pyramids in Egypt.

Spirit beings are an energy form or power in a parallel world to ours, in the same space as us but on different, higher levels of vibration to us. Having no density, they enjoy complete freedom to go wherever they wish to. As mentioned above, they can pass through solid walls at will, without any constraints or restrictions from others or from circumstances.

There is literally nothing to hold them down, whereas in our laboured physical existence, on the lowest possible vibration, we are not free, but very much "a puppet on a string".

Regenerating physical experiences from memories

Since the overriding emotions felt by spirits are love and happiness, they do not feel, for example, physical grief from losing loved ones or the pain of ill health or injury, but instead preserve a memory of just a few seconds of those feelings experienced, maybe long-term, in their human existence. And they do not flinch or recoil during such recollections, however agonising the reality may have been.

Then, if spirits wish to revisit an experience they had in the physical world, they need merely to think about it, in order to recreate and re-enact that reality from memory.

They can for example recreate their earthly memories of tastes such as fine wines, exotic fruit or fish suppers, or of experiences like smoking a cigarette, going on a fairground ride, driving a car or watching a TV programme. Memories live on with each spirit and so continue after physical death, because they are an energy, a vibration, and can be brought back.

When my father-in-law Vic came through to my medium friend Robin on 18th October 2016, Robin could clearly hear the first of the two Henry Cooper – Cassius Clay boxing matches from the 1960s in the background.

Vic was listening with a male neighbour to that live broadcast on a vintage valve radio during a visit to his widowed mother's home in Spring Road, Tyseley, Birmingham. The big fight was taking place on 18th June 1963 in the open air at Wembley Stadium, London, before a noisy crowd of 35,000 which Robin could hear. Such is the extraordinary power of memory and thought!

Our need to measure time & space

All these acts become thought experiences rather than physical experiences. On that basis thoughts are not abstract concepts but living things. In this way our cherished concepts of time and space become "simply tools of the mind". We discuss this later in the context of the American scientist Dr Robert Lanza's take on quantum physics.

Our minds are obliged to devise ways of measuring time and space as tools to manage and regulate our physical world and to organise our own transient existence. There is no such obligation or need in the world of spirit, where eternity and infinity are the natural order.

The stuff of dreams

Thought experiences become more understandable when we reflect that any dream we have whilst asleep in bed seems completely real to us when we are in it, does it not? After we have woken up, it may be considered illusory not real, but at the time we see objects, landscapes and colours – and interact with people and events – because we are altogether part of what is going on in our dream.

Our brain cannot invent a person's face – any face in a dream must be one that we have already seen, however briefly, in life, photos or movies. In a similar vein, places and occurrences that we have once physically experienced, or seen pictured, are absorbed unconsciously by the brain at the time and can be amalgamated irrationally or higgledy-piggledy in a future dream. The mind of a 60-year-old will have unconsciously archived over half-a-million hours of personal experiences.

A dream is our reality within our consciousness at that moment. Different elements in a dream can come from different eras in our memory banks – they are literally "out of time" – because the subconscious mind, like the spirit world, is always "in the now" and does not recognise time.

Dreams can include deep emotions, dealing with loss and reunion, anger, sorrow and fear. Bad dreams and nightmares are among the most startling and emotionally potent of remembered dreams.

Dreams across three depths of sleep

Our dreams may be broken down into three types, at different depths of sleep with different brainwave frequencies that enable synchronisation with spirits' vibrations. The three kinds of dream can be summarised as follows.

Firstly, there are those induced by our subconscious from our everyday thoughts, typically mulling over day-to-day problems or euphoric moments.

Secondly, there are dreams induced or initiated by spirit to our physical minds (where for example departed loved ones come close to us and we get emotional). What are commonly called "visitation dreams" are ones in which loved ones are reaching out to us and communicating with us through our dreams and thereby getting past the filters and obstructions of our waking mind and ego.

For example, when someone who has died comes to visit us in our dreams, we are not going to have the thought from our rational mind that this person is actually dead and should not be in our dream. When they appear, we accept that person's presence without argument.

Thirdly, we have dreams communicated by spirit to our own inner spirit (at the level of the deepest sleep and taking the human mind entirely out of the equation).

Out-of-body experiences & astral travel

The latter type of dream can involve what is known as an "out-of-body experience" (OBE) for our spirit or soul, a journey through the parallel dimension of the astral plane of which the common, physical mind will be unaware. If it were in play, the common mind, as distinct from the subconscious mind, would derail the process through emotions and fear.

So, according to astral projection, our astral or etheric body has the ability to travel widely and independently of its physical counterpart. Anyone is capable of individual and independent mind travel or astral travel within their physical life, providing they can let go of their common mind and ego sufficiently to allow the experience.

Significantly, because time does not exist in the spirit world, this can be a journey for our mind over big distances in the physical past, present or future of our current lifetime – if there is a good enough reason for that.

Whereas a dream can, as we know, involve a full range of human senses and emotions, astral travel does not. You are simply viewing what is in front of you. The concept has in fact been around since ancient times and features in numerous cultures as well as in Books of the Bible.

How brainwaves alter in the course of sleep

Electroencephalography (EEG), monitoring the natural frequency of neural oscillations or brainwaves, shows how amplitude is increased and frequency slowed

States of consciousness

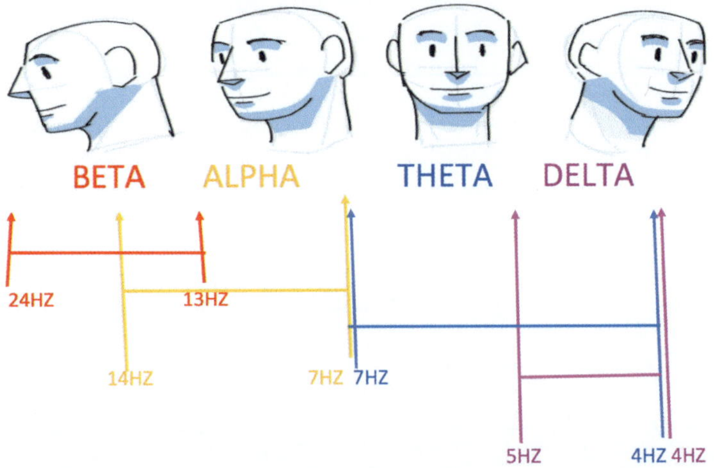

Scientific research into brainwaves shows that each of the four basic Electroencephalography (EEG) waves is linked to a different state of consciousness. The ranges of the waves vary according to which scientific study you look at. The above chart is intended as a guideline only. However, any state of consciousness beyond the Beta state is an entranced state.

The Beta state is a very alert conscious state, whereby the individual is consciously in control.

The Alpha state is a relaxed inspirational state which can include daydreaming or meditation.

The Theta state is compatible with Mediumistical experiences and lighter states of Trance.

The Delta state is associated with the deeper states of Trance, sleep and unconsciousness.

 https://timabbott.net

down during sleep and dream states. That assists communication with the spirit side of life which runs in parallel to ours.

Ultimately any dream whilst asleep, or any daydream, is no more than a series of thoughts created by our mind. By tapping into our subconscious as with thoughts, close loved ones in spirit can in fact put a spirit-induced dream or daydream into our minds as a living energy in order to be part of it, and thereby we pull them closer. Spirits know if you have seen them in your dreams – often making you emotional – but, at the same time, will choose to come into a dream only when it has significance to them.

Unlike us, spirits know the rationale behind any dream we experience. They can also use our dreams to convey awareness of something that we have not noticed or that could happen, and to suggest solutions for wider life problems above and beyond our own needs. Nevertheless we are not constrained by their advice on the "bigger picture" and still have free rein to do what we wish, make our mistakes and learn from them.

The international trance medium and course tutor Tim Abbott assists our understanding of neural oscillations or EEG waves with his diagram above, showing how they vary in Hertz (Hz) frequency for different states of consciousness.

The international trance medium and course tutor Tim Abbott. Instilling in his mediumship students that the appropriateness and the quality of evidence are expressions of the intelligence of spirit, Tim holds diplomas in both demonstrating and teaching platform evidential mediumship over a 35-year career. His practical courses and workshops are in demand in wide-ranging countries from Austria, Canada, Germany and Iceland to New Zealand, Norway, Sweden and Switzerland.

The action of the pineal gland

Tim Abbott is currently researching the role played by mediums' pineal gland when they communicate with the spirit world.

It is an important part of the brain which does most to regulate our daily body clock and sleeping and waking cycles. Producing varying amounts of the hormone melatonin for that purpose, this small, pinecone-shaped gland of our endocrine system is located centrally between the two hemispheres of the brain. The secretion of melatonin is generally inhibited by light and stimulated by darkness, like a photosensitive vestigial or third eye. Therefore its production peaks at night, pointing to the hormone's function regarding sleep.

But the action of the pineal gland also seems to be triggered when the consciousness of mediums becomes passive enough to be able to receive messages from the spirit world by suppressing their common mind, likes, dislikes and ego. By quietening their mind in preparation for spirit communication, they are adjusting the vibrational frequency of their brain. This state-of-mind is analogous to a sleep state.

Intelligence beyond our understanding

In contradiction to what we may egotistically assume, spirit beings or souls as pure intellectual energy have far greater intelligence and vision than we can ever possess. And memories more accurate and detailed than ours of the experiences we shared on the earth plane. They never forget anything and are always able to see that "bigger picture" in life. You can see why mediums as communicators have so much respect for the power of spirit.

Extraordinarily, the personality traits, feelings, opinions and earthly concerns of each individual remain in spirit just as they were last on the earth plane.

Your favourite aunt will still be concerned about the pruning of her azalea shrubs, keeping her house neat and tidy, or whether some family paperwork still has to be sorted – but only as far as these things directly affect us or our environment, or alternatively just to prove spirits' presence around us and the accuracy of their memories.

Spirit knows our future yet cannot tell us

In addition, we humans cannot get past the idea of linear time, which does not exist in the spirit world. To spirit beings, who always see the bigger picture, their future and our future are both happening now, in real time.

Accordingly, in their interactions with the physical world, they can already see the pattern of our future life, and yet cannot betray that to us because it is fundamentally important that we have freewill to make our mistakes, big and small, and hopefully learn from them. As per the old joke, if you knew where you were going to die, you would avoid ever going there, wouldn't you?

Our lifespan as fixed bookends

The beginning and end of our lifespan, like fixed bookends, are pre-planned in support of the immortal spirit form, the soul, within our body. Taking this analogy, bookends which are set close together would mean a short life, bookends widely spaced at varying distances a long life.

However, within that time limitation, as physical beings we have complete freewill to "go our own way" as far as circumstances permit.

In Chapter 14 we discuss further how the boundless intellect of spirit synchronises the totality of time, place and objectives, not to mention future interrelationships and interactions, for each human life like a complex military operation. Yet, whilst there is reasoning behind everything that happens in a life, and it is all integrated and coordinated, this does not deny people the freewill to make their own independent judgements and decisions within that framework.

What is really difficult for us to understand here is that, because of the eternal "Now" – the lack of the time principle – in the spirit dimension, the wider spirit world can see all of our future decisions and actions anyhow, even if our own soul cannot.

The primacy of our personal decisions

If we request their help, spirit can indirectly influence associated people, interactions and events and see to it that we are "in the right place at the right time". However, after we have reached that point, our freewill determines what choice we then make. Arriving at a crossroads in life, it remains entirely our own decision whether we go left, right or straight on. Or even go back to where we missed an earlier turn-off.

The spirit world is fully aware of our future pathway and can (where there is good reason at the time) give us a little insight, a thread of information, tailored to our mental capacity and understanding. And yet spirit is understandably barred from communicating it all to us, because that would feed back and change our future, our behaviour patterns and what we plan to do.

How many Hollywood blockbuster movies have pictured the absurd and unachievable "what if" scenario of travelling back or forward in time, time slip fantasies via a time machine or whatever other method, in order to change the course of history?

What information can the spirit world pass on?

All communicators from spirit are trusted with the knowledge they pass on, and there is no higher authority nor mechanism to enforce this. When we are facing a thorny problem – or going as far as asking for their help – they will offer advice to us, spirit-to-spirit or via a medium.

That advice may include the potential outcomes of alternative courses of action. But how much influence this may, or may not, have on our decisions is entirely down to our judgement and freewill here on the earth plane.

There is no real limit to what the spirit world can tell you, as long as three conditions are met. These are that you and your human contacts are able to understand the information; that it serves a fit and proper purpose; and that advice tendered by spirit is no more than advice.

To underline the point made above, we must always have freewill to display human faults and learn from them in order to enrich our spirit by the experience. That is the whole rationale behind us coming to earth. The spirit is only in the body to live a physical life: it is not there to adjust our life or make us do things.

Nevertheless, whilst "the spirit within" cannot put thoughts into our own mind, other spirits, such as of past family members, can do so, typically to bring us love and comfort or give guidance. Above all, spirits are collectively aware of the innate fears and anxieties burdening each of us as individuals and would never – really never – wish to frighten or hurt us.

In all circumstances they only wish to help and support us as we battle through the ups and downs of our physical lives.

A warning from the spirit world saves my life

A concrete example of advice from spirit, perhaps the ultimate love story. In 2021 my late wife Pam saved my life from the other side by relaying to me a message, which originated from the spirit world, about a future malignant prostate cancer condition. In the absence of any discernible symptoms, I was prompted in consequence to arrange a series of tests in hospital which fully validated this collective warning from the spirit world.

The tests culminated in successful, life-saving prostatectomy surgery which I underwent on 26th October 2021 at the Royal Stoke University Hospital in Newcastle-under-Lyme, England.

Accessing a reservoir of encyclopedic knowledge

As with time and space in the spirit world, the reservoir of knowledge and experience there is limitless. It is like a supercomputer whose memory banks are constantly expanding. Yet it takes up no space because it consists purely of energy and nothing solid. Individual spirits gain greater access to those memory banks as they evolve – with progression and evolvement come greater knowledge and the greater intellectual capacity needed to process it.

The theosophists' term "Akashic Records" – derived from the Sanskrit word Akasha meaning "sky, space or ether" – is misused to mean this central archive of all the information, all the memories, from every individual who has ever lived on the earth. It is in fact nothing physical but refers instead to the monolithic intellect of billions of spirits combined, since the state of "oneness" across the spirit world includes that limitless single reservoir of encyclopedic knowledge.

It contains every deed, word, feeling, thought and intent that have ever occurred at any time in the history of the world and is constantly being updated with every new thought, word or action.

Accordingly, however you look at it, any spirit is going to know far more than we do on the earth plane. Nevertheless some spirits may step forward with personal expertise and experience in specialist subjects such as higher mathematics and physics, cosmology, modern electronics, artificial intelligence and so forth.

Everyone contributes their personal expertise

Each to their own, and everyone contributes! As an aside, I love the story below, given to me in a trance mediumship session by the extremely helpful spirit guide Edward Seymour.

I have interviewed Edward via a trance medium numerous times for the present book, to achieve a better understanding of the spirit world which he inhabits and in particular reincarnation and past lives. Our first discussion took place on January 14th 2018.

On a biographical note, in his physical existence Edward had been a moneyed Old Etonian (an old boy of Eton public school) who had passed away from heart disease in London in 1915 when in his early eighties. Like his brother, a River Thames bridge designer, Edward had studied structural engineering. Socially active in London's gentlemen's clubs, he lived with his wife Mary Jane, son Anthony and daughter

Victoria, supported by half-a-dozen servants, in the Royal Crescent, Holland Park West, in Kensington, London. He predeceased his wife, and both his children grew up to have children of their own.

So Edward's story about how everyone contributes went as follows. In July 1969 Apollo 11 landed on the Moon as the first manned mission to do so. Subsequently the US President Richard Nixon visited the NASA launch site at Cape Canaveral in Florida and spoke to different people on his tour. At one point he stopped to speak to an old black cleaner sweeping the corridors, asking him "Now what do you do here?" The man replied: "Oh, it's quite simple, sir, I help to put a man on the Moon." How true it was that everyone played their part!

Marc L Pittaway

The spirit guide Edward Seymour who had passed with heart disease in London in 1915 in his early eighties

Like a search of the Internet

So, from the shared knowledge pool they can dip into – not dissimilar to searching on key words via an Internet search engine like Bing, Google or Yahoo – spirits can acquaint themselves with say all the world news, technological advances and moral and ethical issues on earth in real time.

They can keep up to speed with politics and parliaments as well as knowledge of smartphones, iPads, driverless vehicles and so forth, irrespective of the generation to which they may have belonged during their stay on earth. If they don't know something, as described earlier they can get advice from specialists whose knowledge is out there.

The permanent knowledge retained by a given spirit is from that spirit's previous lives, whereas "Googled" knowledge is accessed from the supercomputer on a temporary basis and not stored. Much like on our Internet, the latter comprises unlimited information from a vast diversity of sources and the experiences and opinions of millions of others who have gone before.

Yet, being sensitive to our limited intelligence, spirits impart to us only as much as they know we will be able to take in and understand – "we need to learn to walk before we can run". Accordingly they put concepts in terms of what we are able to grasp: we can only understand simplistic, dumbed-down language that relates to what we know and experience on earth.

Sharing thoughts & memories

Via spirit-to-spirit interaction, spirits will pick up on the thoughts of their loved ones here on earth and empathetically know how they feel at any time – whether they are, for example, elated, sad, emotional, stressed or preoccupied with a problem. Feelings are mirrored. Spirits are uplifted if we exhibit zest and passion, downcast if we are stressed, and hate to see us grieving. Equally they like to see how people interact with each other and how their family members are faring with their earthly lives.

The thought process, coupled with the power of love and emotions, can create a far stronger energy than can anything physical.

During a platform demonstration that I witnessed on 21st August 2019 by the professional Derbyshire medium Kathy Grindey, a lady in the audience was visited by the spirit of a six-year-old schoolboy, completely unrelated to her and yet over whom she had been acutely grieving. Hundreds had joined the hunt for the missing boy, Lucas Dobson, who had fallen into a river at Sandwich, Kent, on a family fishing trip and been swept away before his heartbroken father could save him.

The woman in the audience at the Wollaston community village hall in the West Midlands had been distraught at the news report when the little one's body was found. Accordingly her exceptional level of grief from long distance brought him close, both to prove to her that he was now very much alive and well in the spirit dimension, and also perhaps to strengthen her personal faith in spirit.

The link of spirit to spirit being always so strong, the boy had felt the energy generated by the thoughts from the lady's own spirit and reacted to them just four days after losing his mortal life. You could say that all spirits are connected or "plugged in" to each other.

The repercussions of our thoughts

What we think and do on the earth plane will always have repercussions in the spirit world – the two worlds are connected as if by an invisible umbilical cord.

Spirits know what we are thinking about and what our concerns and preoccupations are, such as our reaction to a broadcast or newspaper report when they may share our point-of-view. And they can influence our senses so that we notice more things around us: they can put our eyes in the right direction or stir up a past memory from say a tune that we may hear by chance on the radio or TV.

What is more, as we ponder on a particular memory which attracts a spirit to come close, much like the brightness of a lighthouse attracting moths from afar, that spirit will often bring to our minds further reminiscences in a chain reaction. One thought can lead to another and another.

Spirits also want to keep their memory alive, to be remembered in a sympathetic and favourable way, on the earth plane, as well as to convey love, support, guidance and concern from the other side to their loved ones still here. The thoughts that we send up to them, and the happy personal memories that we share with them, count more than anything to those in spirit.

As stated earlier, the predominant emotions felt by spirits are love and happiness, and other emotions are memories from their past life on earth. To express love and pleasure, they will visualise in front of a medium with a big smile on their face!

Loss of negative earthly emotions

Because spirits are themselves composed entirely of energy, their lives vibrate at a much higher frequency than ours do, and they have lost our negative outward emotional traits, such as fear, frowning, fidgeting, grief, sorrow or shedding tears.

To them, these heavier negative emotions of anger, rage, jealousy, shame, guilt, frustration, yearning, sadness and grief are lower vibrations associated only with human kind, whereas the blissful feelings of love and happiness (lighter positive emotions) are experienced by spirits as energy not now and then but all the time and represent a far higher and faster vibration.

The faster the vibration, the less spirits will feel lower energy. As difficult as it is for us to comprehend this translation of emotions – a concept unfamiliar to our human existence, it lies at the very core of the spirit world.

The depth of love in the spirit world

From a physical perspective it is quite impossible for us to understand and appreciate the depth and strength of love and oneness which exist between spirit entities, who are intrinsically tolerant, non-competitive and non-judgemental. In their blissful, idyllic world, love and happiness, like knowledge and experience, are shared and constantly expanding.

Billions of spirit energies are combined to create that overwhelming, euphoric feeling of love, and our human vocabulary has no term to adequately describe it. As a parallel we might understand, the crowd of over two million for Victor Hugo's funeral procession in Paris (see Chapter 1) were all united by the single thought of their love for the great man, so that huge surge of emotion and affection demonstrated how powerful the emotion of love can be in human terms.

So just how deep can individual love be in the spirit world? In her first book "The Eagle and the Rose", published in 1995 by Warner Books, the international medium and healer Rosemary Altea, born in Leicester, England, in 1946, described the remarkable story of her communication with the spirit of an Aunt Maudie, strangled by her husband, who was imprisoned for her murder.

Although Aunt Maudie's passing had been violent and traumatic, she had been able, with the help of friends and relatives whom she had met in spirit, to refrain from feelings of anger and come to terms with what had happened. Accordingly she bore her husband no malice at all. She explained to Rosemary Altea that in fact she felt very sorry for him.

He was locked up in prison whilst she had all the freedom she could ever want. And whereas she had had the loving arms of her family waiting to comfort her, he now had nobody, for all his remaining family on earth had turned against him, and he was completely without love.

Chapter 3

THE SPIRIT REALM IN HUMAN PERCEPTION

Our obstacles to acceptance

As human beings we are typically very set in our ways and suffer from a general inertia or resistance to experiencing things that seem to be out of the ordinary, out of our comfort zone.

Moreover the rigid framework of rules and regulations surrounding our physical lives can dominate our thinking, to the extent that we may never question authority, depart from orthodoxy nor hold with anything that does not follow convention. And we tend to act far less on impulse as we become older and more careful.

When something has been deeply rooted in our mind over a lifetime as a so-called "core belief", it may be difficult if not impossible to remove it, to unlearn it. Consequently our physical mind can be simply "closed off" and not accept the reality and evidence of the world of spirit. This brings to mind the old adage: "To the believer no proof is necessary, to the non-believer no proof is possible."

But certainly you need to be open-minded and ultimately enter the spirit world with as few preconceptions as possible.

Arguably we have five possible barriers on the earth plane to accepting or understanding the existence of spirits, or the possibility of communication with them:

- our excessive ego and controlling nature;
- our intensely busy minds and lifestyles (family, business, leisure interests and social commitments);
- our lack of intellect, or myopic inability to open our eyes and minds and believe the evidence – where it is conveyed to us by the talk of others rather than proven by personal experience, not dissimilar to "flat earth" versus "round earth" proponents;
- our culture and upbringing, deep-rooted prejudice or inflexible adherence to the tenets of a particular ideology or religion;
- our sheer fear of the supernatural – "things beyond our comfort zone".

Alternatively, the obstacle to our acceptance of the spirit world may comprise an amalgamation of several of the above factors.

Superstition about the supernatural

People can be immensely vulnerable to their own suggestibility. Evil spirits, demons, ghouls, goblins, bogeymen, vampires, zombies, fairies at the bottom of the garden, and suchlike have never existed. These creatures are entirely "constructs of the human mind", products of our over-active imagination, over generations, so the highly experienced spirit guide Alfred tells us, and no genuine medium has ever experienced their presence.

Alfred further insists that a personified God and devil, and an actual heaven and hell, have never existed either, except within humankind's hundreds of traditional belief systems and cultures.

Our cultural fear of the supernatural is a barrier that has been greatly intensified by centuries of misinformed yet cherished folklore, paintings and theatre featuring every character that you can imagine.

This ranges from the three Fates in Greek mythology to Homer's subterranean Underworld of ghosts, from the ghost of Clytemnestra awakening the avenging Furies in Aeschylus to the witch of Endor in the First Book of Samuel. It extends yet further in our culture from the ghost of Hamlet's late father to the three witches and Banquo's ghost in Macbeth, and from Mary Shelley's Frankenstein and Bram Stoker's Count Dracula to Robert Louis Stevenson's Dr Jekyll and Mr Hyde!

Charles Dickens was intrigued by our belief in ghosts and was hugely influential in establishing the popularity of the ghost story genre in the Victorian era. In *A Christmas Carol* published in 1843, the first of his ghost stories, he made the supernatural a natural extension of the real world of the old miser Ebenezer Scrooge and his victims.

Witch trials & executions

On a far more serious level, the absurd myths surrounding witches in Western Europe and Russia alike meant that women accused by superstitious village communities of supernatural hanky-panky had to be eliminated by being drowned or burned alive.

As per the usual test, suspects were thrown by villagers into the local duckpond or moat. It was the ultimate no-win situation. If they sank and drowned, they were adjudged not to be witches, whereas if they floated and survived, they were indeed witches and would be burned at the stake.

During the 16th and 17th centuries a "witch craze" in Europe saw more than 100,000 people accused of witchcraft and executed with the support of the government and often also the church. At that time superstition was rife, and there was hardly any understanding of science or medicine. So if, for example, a person or animal fell ill unexpectedly, it was easy to claim that it had been cursed rather than the issue being disease or poor hygiene. "Witches" were customarily blamed too for crop failures or extreme weather events.

Those denounced as witches tended to be older, poor, single women. They were often picked out because they were different in some way to others, perhaps with unconventional behaviour or appearance, or because someone had a grudge against them.

Europe's biggest witch trials and mass executions took place at Unterzell Monastery in the city of Würzburg, now northern Bavaria, between 1626 and 1631.

Over 900 men and women, some with babes in arms, having been tried and found guilty of sorcery, were tortured and then decapitated or burnt alive. In the general frenzy of accusations, at least 500 executions took place during the same five years in the nearby town of Bamberg too. The victims even included Catholic priests cherished by their community. Those trials ended abruptly when Würzburg was thankfully captured by King Gustavus Adolphus of Sweden in 1631.

Meanwhile witch trials and executions proliferated in 17th century Colonial North America, notably the Salem witch trials of 1692-1693, one of the region's most notorious episodes of Puritan Christian extremism and mass hysteria.

A belief in witchcraft continues to thrive today in some traditional societies, and accusations of witchcraft are the trigger for serious forms of violence including murder, as well as a means of persecuting and abusing women. Such incidents are not uncommon in sub-Saharan African countries as well as in remote rural areas of the Indian subcontinent and Oceania, in countries such as India, Nepal and Papua New Guinea.

For example, in Tanzania, despite the best efforts of its government, albino children living in country areas are still murdered for their body parts on the advice of witch doctors. The objective is to make powerful amulets which are believed to protect against sorcery and make the owner prosper in life and career!

Folklore has become entertainment

In the broader historical context, Egyptian folklore as to the nature of the afterlife goes back over 3,000 years. Many were recorded in hieroglyphic inscriptions, papyrus scrolls and tomb paintings. An ancient Egyptian funerary text, the Book of the Dead, compiles some of the beliefs from early Egyptian history. In modern times, the fanciful concept of a bandaged mummy coming back to life – wreaking vengeance when disturbed in its stone sarcophagus – has spawned a whole genre of horror stories and films.

From the 1790s on, the popularity of phantasmagoria shows using magic lantern projection was a manifestation of people's obsession with the bizarre and the supernatural. In Europe our fascination with the horror movie genre started with German silent productions such as "The Golem", "Nosferatu" and "The Cabinet of Dr Caligari".

The Hollywood effect

Nevertheless the Hollywood entertainment industry must carry most of the blame for its development of sensationalist, over-the-top, Gothic horror and fantasy films, whether aimed at filling cinema seats or latterly selling DVDs and streaming services. Our youngsters in particular get a thrill out of being scared.

There have been some dramatic fictional gems such as "The Exorcist" from William Peter Blatty's 1971 novel, a blockbuster directed by William Friedkin and released in 1973, as well as "The Omen", written by David Seltzer, directed by Richard Donner and first screened in 1976.

But also elaborate inventions have abounded to feed our imagination, such as "The Amityville Horror" released in 1979 as a "true story" and remade in 2005, those two versions together grossing almost $200 million worldwide. But hey, that's entertainment, and, when all is said and done, members of the paying public are not serious enough on a fun night out to be bothered about true life accuracy.

Precognition of major events via a link into a time portal

The impact and energy of a cataclysmic event can be felt as "precognition" even before it happens, and in that way the occurrence can be predicted. Genuine seers and prophets get a snippet or flash of information from the spirit dimension, where there is an eternal Now and therefore future events – echoing H.G. Wells's visionary work "The Shape of Things to Come" – are happening in real time and can be observed.

The soul within these gifted individuals has a thread, a spirit-to-spirit link, into a time portal of the spirit world, as unfathomable as that is for us in the physical world. One can only say that history has shown us numerous examples of such precognition or presentiment, where a soul gets a so-called "Nostradamus insight".

There was the death in June 1559 from jousting of the monarch Henry II of France, foreseen famously by the French visionary Nostradamus two years before it actually occurred.

It duly happened on the day it was meant to, and given his spiritual sensitivity the seer had forewarning of it. However, as in the case of many transformational natural or man-made disasters, his was a lone voice among sceptics, and he could do nothing to stop the accident from happening.

The renowned Bulgarian seer Baba Vanga (1911-96), blind from the age of 12, was held in such high regard that she was visited personally by Soviet and Eastern European leaders and envoys. Her premonitions of forthcoming world events did prove remarkably accurate. She is claimed to have prophesied with over 80% accuracy such occurrences as the dissolution of the Soviet Union, the 9/11 attacks on New York City and Washington, the death of Princess Diana and the 1986 Chernobyl nuclear power plant disaster.

The British celebrity psychic Sally Morgan was another who predicted Princess Diana's fatal car crash at 36 years of age in the Paris road tunnel in August 1997. The black Mercedes S-Class saloon pursued by paparazzi photographers struck a concrete roof-support pillar at excessive speed in the Pont de l'Alma underpass by the River Seine.

Then the September 11th 2001 attack on the Twin Towers of the World Trade Center in New York City was apparently reported to and recorded at local police stations by spiritually aware citizens days before it happened: their warnings were dismissed as baseless and not credible.

In 2008 a book called "End of Days" by Sylvia Celeste Browne, a medium who was born in Kansas City and lived from 1936 to 2013, foresaw that: "In around 2020 a severe pneumonia-like illness will spread throughout the globe, attacking the lungs and the bronchial tubes and resisting all known treatments."

In December 2019 a new and highly infectious respiratory disease was identified by health authorities in the city of Wuhan on the Yangtze River in central China. The sickness was soon discovered to be caused by a novel strain of coronavirus known as Covid-19.

The virus had most likely escaped from a virology laboratory in Wuhan researching pathogens being carried by flying bat species from Chinese caves. Evolving strains have now spread around the world as a pandemic and killed millions of people, the hardest hit countries including the USA, UK, Russia, Brazil, Mexico, India and Italy.

Just as Sylvia Browne foretold, the disease attacks the respiratory system and there is currently no known cure. The spirit world knew exactly that this pandemic would arise and sweep the world, but equally knew that nothing could stop it.

So, whilst it is only natural to harbour doubts as to the validity of some predictions and prophecies, the general weight of evidence from the multiplicity of sources over history supports the hypothesis of "precognition" from the spirit dimension.

Residual energy from a past tragedy

On a psychic level, the vibration of residual energy from a past tragedy can still have great physical impact.

My medium friend Robin once had the distinct feeling that someone had previously passed away in a taxi in which he was travelling, and it proved upon checking to be absolutely true. There again, when unofficially called in on occasions and listened to, "psychic detectives" have been able to render unique assistance to police departments, notably in the USA, UK and Australasia, with tracking down missing persons, dead bodies and murderers.

An event is an experience which is an "energy in time". The energy from a death has a lasting effect, associated with finality and irrevocability. It stops at the place where it occurs and is soaked up into the earth. The traits of human energy (from blood, guts and gore if you like) remain as residue in the ground, whereas eternal soul energy moves on with the natural process of transition.

That contrasts with non-spiritual, euphoric energies, generated typically by mass gatherings or entertainments, which are largely taken home at the end by living participants and persist in their memories.

Quantum physics theory debunks the idea of death

Such tapping into the residual energy present in an environment, or on an object, to discover historical information is called psychometry. It is an aspect of quantum physics, a theory in physics based upon the proposition that energy comprises a stream of tiny particles.

The trailblazer Max Planck had first named tiny energy packets as quantums, and his fellow German Albert Einstein theorised that the energy in a beam of light actually consists of individual particles, now called photons. Stephen Hawking went on to show that all-devouring black holes in space, with their intense gravitational fields, must leak particles of light and other radiation, linking the classical theory of gravity directly with quantum theory.

So quantum physics, also known as quantum mechanics or quantum theory, is the science of the very small. It explains the often highly unusual behaviour of matter and its interactions with energy at the scale of the molecules, atoms, ions and sub-atomic particles that form and govern our world.

The relationship with the world of nature is well described for the layman by the theoretical physicist, author and broadcaster Professor Jim Al-Khalili, OBE, FRS, in his YouTube video "The Secrets of Quantum Physics – Let There Be Life":

https://youtu.be/q4ONRJ1kTdA

In contrast to quantum physics, classical Newtonian physics is limited to explaining matter and energy on a scale familiar merely to human observation and experience, that is at regular, macroscopic scale. It spells out how macroscopic objects, from projectiles to machinery to satellites, move and how gravity works. Yet there is a convincing argument that the micro view, even if it is less immediately recognisable, should have precedence over the better known macro one.

Adjudged in 2014 one of Time Magazine's 100 Most Influential People in the World, a leading US biologist, stem cell researcher and doctor of medicine Robert Lanza maintains that the theory of biocentrism inherent in quantum physics or quantum mechanics teaches us that death as we know it is an illusion, a figment of our imagination. Check out his reasoning in two YouTube videos:

https://youtu.be/WFjGz28yTQ0

https://youtu.be/BZ6MIk8-pSA

Dr Robert Lanza (born 1956 in Boston, Mass.) **www.bostonglobe.com**

Biocentrism & our consciousness

In various books and scientific papers Dr Lanza argues that our biological consciousness constructs the universe and visual reality around us rather than being a by-product of them. Biocentrism theory explains that the universe exists only because of an individual's consciousness of it – essentially life and biology of any kind are central to reality, which in turn creates the universe: the universe itself does not create life.

The same applies to the concepts of space and time, which Lanza describes as "simply tools of the mind". As discussed above in Chapter 2, Einstein's Theory postulates that there is no such thing as absolute time, and that time and space are always relative to the observer. Lanza takes this one step further, contending that the human observer actually creates time.

Limitations to our sensory perception

Of course seeing is not necessarily believing, although our mind thinks that it is. In reality the brain tells the eyes what we see. Cognitive neuroscience raises the question "what is reality?"

To make sense of the world it is necessary to organise incoming sensory signals into information which is meaningful. We have all come across optical illusions such as visual puzzles and impossible objects. Our brain according to Gestalt principles of perception can make sense of these bizarre images and effects only by trying to rationalise and organise them and fit them together into a pattern more familiar to us.

Computer-generated imagery (CGI) and 3D visualisations create illusions with sound and vision in movies, TV programmes, videos, video games, commercials and simulators all the time in the modern era. And of course film animation has always been based on the illusion that the brain perceives a series of slightly varied images produced in rapid succession as a moving picture.

The human eye sees its surroundings not continuously but only in frames per second. We may be aware of the refresh rate in Hertz of our TV screen and will notice for example if a projector film, an old silent movie or a computer game flickers or stutters. Indeed some films and games create the special effect of "motion blur" at so many frames per second.

Colours we can see & cannot see

Faster than sound, light travels outward as transverse waves, vibrating from side to side, from the source that has created it. However, visible light emanates from only the part of the electromagnetic spectrum perceivable by the human eye.

The shorter the wavelength, the higher are the frequency and energy. Visible light is generally defined as having wavelengths in the narrow spectrum of 400 to 700 nanometres (nm), from violet to red, sandwiched between short-wavelength invisible ultraviolet (UV) and invisible infrared (IR) with long wavelengths. This range corresponds to electromagnetic wave frequencies of approximately 750 down to 430 terahertz (THz).

However, there are animal species such as birds and insects well able to detect more frequencies and colours than we can. Hence we use UV light for traps which attract and kill flying insect pests.

Regardless of the limited range of colours and vibrational frequencies that we ourselves are able to physically detect, our ability to select one colour over another means that arguably we also have an unconscious ability to base our choice upon the difference in their two vibrations. Accordingly, a common method of creating the reality we want around us could be to use colours which align with our preferred vibrations.

Colours correspond to different energy centres in the body called chakras, which we discuss in Chapter 12. Each chakra of the body balances, stores and distributes the energy needed for life.

Illustrating the vibrational frequencies of colours within visible light from violet to red. The identical spectrum of colours is found in rainbows, the dispersal of natural white light as it passes through a triangular prism, and energy centres of the human body called chakras.

Where seeing is not believing

The eye is no camera, and the brain is no computer, so that they can only pick up on certain elements in their field of vision at any one time, whether familiar things or unusual things.

Then, when you look straight ahead, it's not the same experience as with the sides of your eyes, which are more sensitive to brightness and to flickering. Moreover a bright stimulus will as we know leave a physiological afterimage behind on the retina.

What is more, our eyes may have different sensitivities to different colours across the spectrum, whilst some of us are colour blind. Red-green is the most common form, followed by blue-yellow colour blindness and total colour blindness. Then older people often suffer from age-related retinal defects, affecting what they see.

Also relevant to our discussion is the Charles Bonnet syndrome, well documented by the UK National Health Service (NHS), Royal National Institute of Blind People (RNIB) and World Health Organization (WHO) as being unrelated to mental health problems or dementia. This is where visually impaired or wholly blind people – possibly to compensate for their disability – see hallucinatory visions of events, people or places in full detail. We cannot be sure whether this phenomenon is physiologically or spirit related.

Furthermore we can simply look and fail to notice: for various reasons an innocent, guileless and curious child, with uncluttered, unprogrammed mind, will generally notice far more about its surroundings than an adult.

Another significant point is that under some circumstances the human brain, mind or ego is so powerful that it can affect the senses rather than the other way around: the interaction can be two-way. The mind can block senses such as, for example, the sense of smell, so that in daily life you possess no sense of smell, unless you are in an altered state as a medium – when spirit may employ that sense in order to communicate.

And yet our sensory perception, despite this catalogue of such obvious, serious limitations, shapes our consciousness of the outside world!

Personal reality is shaped by the mind

To quote from "Beyond Biocentrism", a book co-written by Robert Lanza and the American astronomer and science populariser Bob Berman: "Reality is an active process that always involves our consciousness. Everything we see and experience is a whirl of information occurring in our minds, shaped by algorithms that create brightness, depth, and a sense of time and space. Even in dreams, our mind can assemble information into a 4D spatiotemporal experience."

Lanza goes on to explain that, according to this theory, the concept of death "cannot exist in any real sense", since there are no true boundaries by which to define it, and passing consists purely of a thought. Essentially, the idea of dying is something we have long been taught to accept, he says, but in reality it exists only within our minds.

Accordingly consciousness survives and lives on, which is very much the message of this book. And how you conceive and create your own personal reality – your virtual reality – through that consciousness is the key to your future development.

Chapter 4

SO WHAT IS LIFE LIKE IN THE SPIRIT REALM?

Energy forms in a parallel world

As I have said earlier, spirit beings are an energy form or power in a parallel world to ours, living in the same space as us but on higher vibrations than ours.

They may choose to observe, stay close to and support their surviving loved ones on this earth plane, but for perhaps only a quarter of their time, when they are not learning and progressing in the spirit world, as higher energies on a higher vibration. Co-existing with us, spirit entities are not a physical being but a consciousness, and exist forever.

Just as indestructible energy in the physical world can convert into many things, so spirit beings consisting of raw energy can assume many guises. They can present themselves to us at whatever age they choose, and in whatever clothes, from their lives on the earth plane.

Because that body is a projection from their soul, they can alter it as they see fit. Clothing is made out of light, not fabric. But, if at all possible, they will appear to evidential mediums in a familiar form which is going to be recognised, to give context and authority to their messages.

Nevertheless one spirit sees another spirit as pure energy and not as David Bowie, Karl Lagerfeld, Karl Marx or whoever they may have been in their last life on earth.

Spirits suffer neither pain nor ailments, because, once they are free of their physical body, they can feel no pains or disabilities. They don't need to eat, and require no buildings or streets to live in on the spiritual plane.

However, much as we do, at times they will in fact go into a complete state of rest – helping them to regenerate and replenish their energy and stay strong.

They need that energy to perform many tasks such as travelling long distances in a flash and interacting with us in many different ways in the physical world, for instance providing non-physical healing. Spirits on a higher and finer vibration level possess a greater amount of this natural energy and ability to accomplish things.

Around spirits are the bright and vivid colours of other energy forms, but no days, nights, months, years and seasons. Spirit beings are unaffected by light and darkness, heat and cold, or weather conditions, because such physical environmental factors are irrelevant to their dimension. To them any human, animal, plant, leaf or tree is an energy form, glowing rather than in physical outline.

Energy working invisibly

Vision is, however, not relevant to the spirit world. You cannot see energy there in any conventional way, but merely its effects.

Similarly on the earth plane, you can see the invisible energy of a magnet only by how it attracts iron filings – or electricity only when, for instance, it lights up your house or street. Then electromagnetic interference can, as we know, occur unseen between one electrical device and another close by. Microwave, X-ray and infrared are further forms of unseen energy which are part and parcel of modern technology.

Alternatively, think of the energy produced by your exhaled breath. It is there, but you can never see it, except on a cold morning. Just consider too the impact of strong winds or the many colourless gases around us that can nevertheless have powerful effects.

Moving at the speed of thought

Energy can travel so fast: there is nothing to stop it. So, as concentrated energy, spirits can move about instantaneously, at the speed of thought. Flying with freedom and joy through time from one state of existence to another, "letting go of the physical", spirits have no boundaries.

They can whizz "here, there and everywhere" in a split second, the blink of an eye, like J.M. Barrie's characters Peter Pan and Tinker Bell, although cannot be in two places absolutely simultaneously.

On what would have been our 36th wedding anniversary in 2019, my late wife Pam did make me laugh when she said: "I may not be able to pick up a chip from a plate any longer, but I can be in Australia in a nanosecond, so there!"

Another thing spirits cannot do is to move up to a faster and finer vibration than the one they merit, because higher levels of personal enlightenment, the realms of lighter and brighter energies, are to be reached only through learning appropriate lessons and expanding wisdom through experience.

Travelling to unknown locations

Apart from anything else, this extreme freedom and flexibility enable spirits to be well up-to-date with what is happening in a host of places. Where they see a good reason for it, they can travel to locations around the earth to which they have never been physically. They can be invited and drawn to visit a compatible fellow spirit residing within a person anywhere in the physical world without knowing their address.

Nearer at hand, the more inquisitive ones will follow closely everything that is happening within their family or circle of friends remaining behind on the earth plane. Drawn in by the love and affection they feel towards the occupants, spirits may choose to stay with them in their house for much of the time.

In the spirit realm, all your senses and emotions such as love and bliss are heightened to a much greater degree than they are on earth. There exists a different sort of love, far stronger there and more intense, emanating from a far higher vibration than in our world. Fundamentally, spirit life is a great deal happier than earth life.

"Becoming one" with other souls

On "coming home" to the spirit world, you learn to "live as one" with other spirits or souls – with a complete absence of divisive human emotions such as hatred, anger, greed, distrust, jealousy or envy.

You are left with only memories from your physical life of such destructive emotions. In the world of spirit, everything works together in unison, and every spirit will help every other spirit.

What is meant by the term "God"?

The fusion of all spirit energies into the "oneness" of the spirit world comprises what we, in human parlance, might describe as the God force or the Great or Greater Spirit. It is the sum total of all those energies put together. As the source of all life, it permeates, feeds and nurtures everything that is life: everywhere where there is life, the God force or Greater Spirit is present.

A monotheistic single deity is not directing everything from on high, although it can comfort us greatly in human terms to make that our reality. Many people have always held firm to the concept of an immortal, omniscient and omnipotent celestial being – God, Jehovah, Yahweh, Allah or Buddha, in previous cultures perhaps Amun-Ra, Jupiter, Odin or Zeus – sitting on a gilded throne and governing all human affairs.

Here I am reminded of words from the landmark anti-war play "Mother Courage and Her Children", written in 1939 by the avant-garde German dramatist Bertolt Brecht. They are "Der Mensch denkt: Gott lenkt", which may be translated as "Man imagines that God is in charge".

Fusing into a molecular structure

You are never alone in the spirit world and, by "living as one", you share and absorb knowledge taken from each other's experiences and memories. It is a process or continuum of "becoming one", much like coalescing or fusing into a molecular structure.

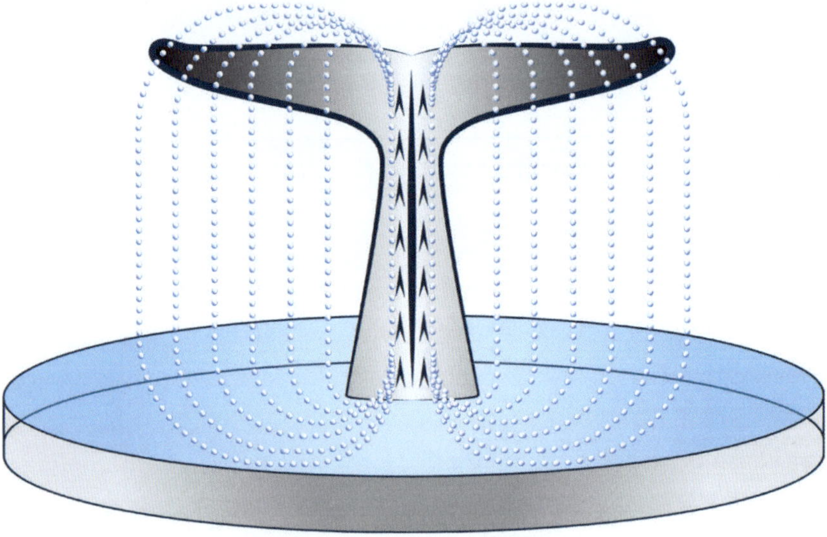

The whale tail fountain

The whale tail fountain represents the continuous cycle of life and rebirth for the soul or spirit.

Each droplet is an individual soul which, upon physical death, returns to the basin to become part of the universal whole as it was before, whilst retaining the individuality, memories and concerns of its immediate past life.

Thereafter, having freewill, the soul has the opportunity to recirculate upwards or, in spirit terms, reincarnate and be born into a completely fresh life.

That new life can allow the soul to learn the further lessons it needs for its evolvement towards greater understanding and enlightenment and faster and finer vibrations.

As illustrated above, another analogy is how an individual soul's life falls as one of the multitude of droplets from the top of a fountain, to become part of the whole body of water in the basin below, and may then recirculate anew, or in spirit terms reincarnate.

And yet, returning to the universal whole or assembly of spirits on the demise of its physical body, the soul never loses the individuality, memories and concerns of its immediate past life on earth. Personality and intelligence live on.

Competitiveness & self-aggrandisement

The concept of "oneness" so described is the very opposite to defining and accentuating yourself as a separate persona in the physical world, where, increasingly in modern times, we cannot "live as one". We live fundamentally as individuals. We do not naturally join together and work side-by-side in order to help and support the neediest around us.

Instead, many of us regard conflict, "win-at-all-costs" competitiveness and self-aggrandisement as being essential to "the survival of the fittest" and the acquisition of strength and supremacy in a money- and power-orientated world where Social Darwinism rules OK.

Such a world is a breeding-ground for sociopaths, who lack remorse and shame, are manipulative and never accept responsibility for their actions. These individuals exist for themselves and only for themselves, disregarding the feelings of others. Lacking all sense of moral responsibility and social conscience, many will achieve positions of power by virtue of their ruthless behaviour. Tyrants ruling nations with an iron fist invariably show no pity, no compassion and no understanding of what the victims of war and deprivation suffer.

Unrestrained greed and narcissistic love of the self has been portrayed in so many of our books, plays and films – from numerous Greek and Shakespearian tragedies to Hollywood classics like Oliver Stone's "Wall Street" in 1987. For his authentic role in that film as the ruthless, heartless, self-obsessed financier Gordon Gekko, Michael Douglas won the Best Actor Oscar at the 60th annual Academy Awards in 1988.

Altruistic perspective of the spirit world

With the exception of pockets of the population, the richest and most developed countries in the world are generally the farthest from nature and the poorest in spirituality and community spirit. By contrast, people in poverty-stricken countries, or those inspired by a "Dunkirk spirit" during wartime, are forced by circumstances to pull together and help each other in order to survive.

Darwinians would argue that reciprocal altruism is in play here, when selfless actions are performed only because they increase the likelihood of repayment in the future. However, if your survival is under immediate threat, say with bombs dropping around your ears in the London Blitz, then you pull together very strongly as a community and harbour no great expectations for the future.

In the extreme case of Gordon Gekko, his "mind, body and spirit" are not working in unison but have drifted far apart from each other, and there is a sharp divide between exterior persona and soul or spirit, the eternal higher self which is resident in the physical body. Then the persona with its negative human traits holds sway over the soul, and you could say that the individual becomes literally "soul-less", losing every shred of loving-kindness towards fellow human beings.

The egotistic, "I'm all right Jack" attitude and code of ethics based on the self – selfishness if you will – rather than on the "oneness" of the collective are diametrically opposed to the altruistic perspective of the spirit world that man's moral duty is to live for others, to give without receiving.

In that world, unlike ours, power, riches and social status mean absolutely nothing. As we all know, you cannot take your wealth with you. Pure lust for power is a human failing that corrupts our world and sows disunity and enmity. To quote the famous words of Jimi Hendrix, which originated with Mahatma Gandhi: "When the power of love overcomes the love of power, the world will know peace."

Your soul casts off your physical body

We ourselves are a spirit or soul in a physical body. The spirit becomes what may be termed as "the soul" when it is resident in a physical body. Whereas the physical form is bound by nature to change and age, the spirit form, the soul within, does not change at all.

Moreover the soul can at times exist at a distance from that body and yet still be connected to it. Indeed, an out-of-body experience (OBE), the experience of a spirit leaving its human body and consciously observing it from a detached perspective, can occur during dreams – or close to a person's passing as a near-death experience (NDE).

Research conducted at the University of Virginia

The expert academic on this subject has been Dr Bruce Greyson, Emeritus Professor in the faculty of Psychiatry and Neurobehavioral Sciences at the University of Virginia in Charlottesville. He has investigated over 1000 cases of NDEs.

Watch this 2018 YouTube panel discussion at the University of Virginia, moderated by John Cleese, in which Greyson and his academic research group, the Division of Perceptual Studies, participated:

https://youtu.be/4RGizqsLumo

Dr Bruce Greyson, University of Virginia

www.vabook.org

Research Professor Edward F Kelly, University of Virginia

www.med.virginia.edu

Another member of the panel that day, Edward Francis Kelly, Research Professor in Bruce Greyson's faculty, is the lead author of two scholarly, collaborative works, "Irreducible Mind: Toward a Psychology for the 21st Century" (2007) followed by "Beyond Physicalism: Toward Reconciliation of Science and Spirituality" (2015), both of which aim to integrate science and the spiritual into an internally consistent world view.

The first tome of 800 pages documents academic research supporting the premise that consciousness is far more than just a product of neural activity. It is shown by evidence to exist independently of the brain or body, with which it causally interacts during physical life but the death of which it survives. Essentially the brain functions only as a transmitter of consciousness, similar to a radio, and not its originator, a general misconception.

Ed Kelly's other book, of over 600 pages, is the product of a 15-year collaboration with a multidisciplinary team of specialists including physicists, neuroscientists, psychiatrists, psychologists, parapsychologists and anthropologists.

Near-death experiences

In a particularly compelling video, subsequent to awaking from a coma lasting nine days, a German lady, Anke Evertz from Greding in central Bavaria, is interviewed on her near-death experience:

https://youtu.be/O2whJPweTkQ

When her clothing caught fire in an horrific accident in the lounge of her apartment, Anke was taken out of her burning body and watched the incident neutrally and unconnectedly from two metres away. Over the nine days of her coma, she soon realised that she could not only apprehend everything which the intensive care doctors around her hospital bed in Munich were thinking and feeling, but also move effortlessly through any solid surface.

In near-death experiences, many people have indeed reported finding themselves floating weightlessly near the ceiling of their hospital room, calmly watching the medics below desperately trying to resuscitate them. And yet the spirit never leaves a body for good until all life has been extinguished in that body, and the individual is clinically dead.

Energy flows from the soul to animate the body. The body is like an overcoat, outer shell or chrysalis that your soul casts off as you "die" and make your transition into an unphysical life or "cross the stream". Another analogy is that of the spirit breaking out of the eggshell of its spent physical body.

In an instant you move from the incarnate to the discarnate state, from a physical family to a non-physical one which exists on a different vibrational frequency. Your past family, friends and pet animals who loved you are calling you and waiting to celebrate your homecoming on the other side. When our nearest and dearest pass away, the supreme irony is that their ancestors celebrate, whilst we grieve!

Importantly, in the spirit world you don't "see" your family and friends, but you feel them, you know they are there. It is a beautiful experience quite beyond our earthly comprehension. It is like going back inside the womb, accentuating the feelings of love, peace and safety. Fellow spirits around you will be people from your past, people whose lives you have touched significantly in some way, however briefly. Just how many lives have you touched or had a positive effect upon?

A representation of how the soul or spirit leaves the body after a person's clinical death

Chapter 5

HOW THIS WILL AFFECT US

Our interactions with spirit & "the tour"

Where we have a terminal illness, existing spirits will come closer and closer, and their love (a stronger pull than earthly love) becomes stronger and stronger as the malady progresses, to take away the fear of passing when it eventually comes.

It happened with my mother Gwen in the last three days before she passed in February 2001 at 85 with bowel cancer in the former Marie Curie Warren Pearl hospice, Solihull. Her spirit guide, a teenage Scottish girl called Mary-Ann McDougall, took her in a deep dream state on several tours to meet relatives and friends from the past.

The latter are always people in whose company you are going to feel safe and comfortable, to put you at your ease. Such a tour by your spirit guide is recorded by either your conscious or subconscious mind and is tailored to your comprehension of physicality and non-physicality and to your degree of open-mindedness. I explain about spirit guides in Chapter 16.

Mary-Ann had lived with her family at a croft, a small rented cattle farm of a few acres, in the rural Scottish Highlands towards Aberdeen and died young in 1837. From her dwelling, which was quite high up, the North Sea was visible.

The journeys that my mother undertook with Mary-Ann were from one state of existence to another, as out-of-body experiences – mind travel – to give her peace-of-mind and reassurance that there were better things, a better life, to come. The initial journey was less strong and intense, more like a living dream in which she met just a couple of her past loved ones.

My mother has likened such a tour to the dream-like experience of appearing in a movie whilst simultaneously watching it! Emotions and feelings are part and parcel of it, whereas astral travel as discussed in Chapter 2 is devoid of those things.

The same spirit guide Mary-Ann had supported her, and interacted with her, 80 years before, when my mother had been on the danger list with scarlet fever for several months between the ages of four and five. Although the disease was a major cause of death in children of that era, the guide reassured her spiritually through her dreams that she would survive it, and indeed she did.

Currently Mary-Ann is back in the spirit world, without a human host but on an

A coming-of-age photo of my mother Gwen Haines wearing real pearls popular at the time, in front of an artistic backdrop, taken in a small, recommended studio outside Wolverhampton, shortly before her 21st birthday which was on March 10th 1936

extremely high vibration, down to her great experience and many lives. She may not wish to return again to the earth plane, often perceived wryly by the spirit world as "a form of punishment"!

Then, prior to her passing in February 2014 from an advanced, aggressive, ovarian cancer, my wife's soul was taken on several tours by one of her two spirit guides, a minor tribal leader mentioned in the Old Testament. He used to lead his nomadic tribe many miles across the deserts of the Holy Land to find fresh grazing for their livestock, a large flock of sheep and goats. Holding a traditional staff, he is a tall and slim male who appears as loving and very wise. He had four brothers, and he passed to spirit in his 50s.

But other members of my wife's family in spirit would also have participated in her tours, in order to enrich her experience through their presence.

Such interactions with spirit help to remove the natural fear factor and to achieve an acceptance of the life that will follow physical death.

Clearly the tour of the afterlife, generally conducted by a spirit guide or past relatives, can only take place if a passing can be foreseen, typically with a terminal illness. It is not possible in the case of a sudden death by accident, killing or suicide, where people equally have no chance to "say goodbye" to their loved ones.

Our own transition to the spirit world

Forget the popular mythology when you pass of going through the pearly gates of heaven, alongside angels reclining on clouds strumming their harps!

Indeed, our traditional cultural idea of "heaven and hell" from Dante's Inferno (the 14th century Italian poem about the nine circles of hell) and from the Sistine Chapel ceiling, painted by Michelangelo between 1508 and 1512 and one of the most renowned artworks of the High Renaissance, does not correspond with any reality. And nor does the right-hand panel, the Last Judgement hellscape, of triptychs by Dutch master Hieronymus Bosch or Flemish painter Hans Memling from the same era.

A century-and-a-half later, along similar lines, we have John Milton's epic poem in blank verse "Paradise Lost", the Biblical story of the Fall of Man, in which the capital of Hell is amusingly called Pandemonium, a place where you are presumably knee-deep in all the demons from the Sistine Chapel ceiling!

In truth, the experience of transition should hold no fear for anyone, whether you are prepared for it or not. It is as easy and simple as falling asleep and then waking up. Our spirit body slips out of our physical body, taking the mind with it, and we awake to our new surroundings to find our past loved ones ready to help and instruct us in our new life. The action of passing is simply the severance of this spirit body from the physical body.

Euphoric feeling of love & happiness

Transition is universally described as the upsurge of an euphoric feeling, a surge of electricity, with an overwhelming, intense feeling of love and elation and of being wanted, accompanied by an instantaneous brightness and radiance. You are carried along by it all and progress in a split second from the physical to a new spiritual reality, which can only be described as a paradise or permanent state of bliss, a state of perfection.

At the moment of physical death, the individual will typically experience a bright light filling the room or immediate area, and any humans present will gradually fade and be replaced by spirit energies of the closest past loved ones and friends waiting to "meet and greet" the so-called deceased.

A couple of spirits present at the moment of transition can instantly summon up a whole crowd. Another scenario of transition is the experience of moving at speed, like a train going through a tunnel, with relatives and friends lining the way, towards a brightly lit destination you are approaching.

The "meet and greet" experience & beyond

Those who had the strongest emotional connection to you, whether over a longer or shorter period, will be the two or three at the front of a crowd, as at the apex of a snooker ball triangle or under the spotlights of a stage in front of a theatre audience. That audience is progressively staggered in importance as you peer towards those dimmer and less decipherable figures ranged at the back.

Spirits will present themselves in the particular persona, stage of life and dress in which they themselves felt happiest and most comfortable and which are most familiar to the person making the transition. In some cases spirits will delay embarking on a new life because they are waiting patiently to meet and greet someone who has not yet passed over.

Everyone, without exception, will have someone waiting to welcome them with the essence of love. This fact has been confirmed to me again and again by the spirit community. You can easily be met by previous generations of your family whom you never knew on the earth plane – or by past friends and acquaintances over whatever timespan. Animals such as pets which have significantly touched your life and your spirit will be in the gathering too. It is like a big party where you, as the new entrant to the spirit world, are the centre of attention.

The degree of spiritual compatibility, or of positive spiritual interaction and impact, in your past human life determines who is at your welcoming party. Who has wanted and loved you the most? Which people and animals have you been closest to and happiest with?

The more spirits who meet you, the easier, more comfortable and more loved you feel and the faster your mental acceptance of your physical death and transition to spirit will be. It is naturally hard to believe in something that you never thought existed.

When death appears to be the natural consequence of a lengthy terminal illness, you are more prepared for it psychologically. The seeds have already been planted in your subconscious. But, in the case of a sudden and unexpected passing without foreknowledge, from say an accident, then your transition is a greater shock to the system and your understanding of your new situation is far less.

Adjusting to your new existence

In the "meet and greet" phase, you see loved ones initially in their familiar physical form, so that you can recognise who they are. Then, as you gradually lose your own physicality, you progress to see their energetic form – their form as a being composed entirely of an indestructible orb of energy.

From that point on, you just "know" that your loved ones are around you, and that state of "knowing" is too unfamiliar a concept for us humans to grasp. There is a huge perceptional change from the earthly state and the physical body to spirit.

As the physical body, the husk or vessel which carries the spirit, perishes, you move to your new spiritual reality and acquire an overwhelming feeling of love, peace and freedom, leaving all existing infirmities, symptoms and diseases behind.

In summary, the vital point in all this is the mental acceptance of the experience of death, transition and the whole new existence that will follow for everyone.

Non-believers who are convinced that "When you're dead, you're dead" get their point-of-view challenged immediately they enter the spirit world. They are faced with the question of how soon, quickly or slowly, will they accept their transition and the new reality in which they necessarily find themselves. Others after their passing to spirit have emotional issues to work out, before moving on and possibly coming through to a medium.

The activities of rescue circles

A rescue circle is a group of spiritualists known as lightworkers, usually sitting together on a regular basis, who spend their time connecting with spirits whom they believe are having difficulty adjusting to the transition from life on the physical plane to life on the spiritual one. Powerful emotional empathy towards others and a determination to help them are the common traits of lightworkers.

Allegedly, the surviving human consciousness and personality can in some cases prevent individuals from accepting their own passing and their new reality to the extent that they prefer to remain in physical locations with which they are familiar. They can neither accept the existence of spirits nor imagine anything other than the physical world and get doubly frustrated that humans in that world can no longer recognise their presence.

This dilemma may have been brought about by a traumatic event such as their sudden and unexpected demise, deep-seated religious dogmatism, or a variety of reasons tying them to their old life. The logic is that, if the sitters, the lightworkers, in the rescue circle are able to connect with the spirit and explain what has transpired, and how spirits are meant to progress to the next stage, then that spirit – held up as it were in human time between two worlds – can continue on its journey.

Amongst the earliest documented examples was the Buffalo rescue circle in upstate New York between 1875 and 1900. Then, in his 1921 work "Wanderings of a Spiritualist", Sir Arthur Conan Doyle detailed the work of the Tozer rescue circle whom he had visited in Melbourne, Australia, the previous year.

However, although a rescue circle has absolutely the best intentions to ease the process of transition and encourage the spirit being to "go to the light within itself", others would contend that spirits eventually move on and migrate to the spirit world whatever the circle does. When that full transition has taken place, the spirit entity will then banish its earthly hang-ups and prejudices and accept its new life in spirit.

The "life review" reflects upon your decisions & actions

Following successful transition, a video of your entire life, a so-called "life review", is replayed to you in what may seem to be a short time. It is a full colour, three-dimensional, panoramic review from a third-person perspective that, with the absence of time in the spirit world, is not presented in calendar order as we knew it. It is played out multi-dimensionally like a hologram and not chronologically, with time and space playing no role.

The review considers what sort of life you have lived, spiritual or otherwise, what you have done and left undone, and the happiness or unhappiness you have brought to the lives of others. It looks back on your decisions and actions at particular times which have affected other lives, human and animal, what you have learned in your life, and how your soul has progressed and evolved spiritually as a result.

If for instance you see yourself committing a self-interested, hurtful or malicious act, then you are transported into the consciousness of the sufferer, so that you feel his or her sadness, sorrow and hurt. In contrast, you will experience the happy feelings engendered in the recipient by a caring and warm-hearted act of yours.

If you have taken revenge for a loss that you have suffered at people's hands, then, looking through their eyes at the bigger picture, what factors drove them to inflict that damage on you?

Being shown the wider effects of your actions

The knock-on effect of your decisions and actions on the lives of people around you and their families, the chain reaction be it good or bad, is described, so that you come to realise the wider ramifications of what you have done or what has befallen you in your physical life.

Your understanding of such a chain reaction becomes clearer because, in your new state, your energy will have merged with, and become one with, that of other spirits close to you emotionally.

In the course of your life review, the sharing of memories, experiences and emotions with the closest loved one who has been there to meet and greet you allows you both to evolve spiritually.

Even a baby who has passed before birth and never touched the earth will experience a review of its life, having been connected with the energy of its mother, family and household.

The soul from the shortest human lives learns that its host has been loved by parents and family and discovers what impact the transition has had upon those people. By far the biggest lesson here is for the bereaved mother to understand how to let go of her uniquely felt, overwhelming love for her child who did not survive.

Neither moral judgement nor punishment

This "story of your life" focuses on your life choices. It shows how you have enriched the lives of others, or what injuries and wrongs you have inflicted on them and may later have regretted, pointing out "the error of your ways". But it also reveals your emotions when people close to you have suffered greatly or passed over.

Through this debrief, the physical part of your spirit sees the events of your life from a different, third-person and objective standpoint, with character flaws and all. You are given the opportunity to consider and understand why you've done what you've done in your life, so that you can improve and move forward as a spirit. You judge your own physical shortcomings in order to move on and become better in future. Conscience, being a human trait, does not come into it.

In fact the life review leads neither to moral judgement by others nor to any particular punishment or karmic retribution.

A fundamental principle of the spirit world is that blame is never apportioned, quite different to the physical world where proven guilt attracts punishment. Furthermore how can you possibly punish an immortal spirit energy which lacks human emotions and a physical body by inflicting pain, dispossession, imprisonment, capital punishment and so forth?

The reasoning by spirit is that, however bad you may have been in your life, there are going to be extenuating circumstances, underlying causality for your actions – your genes, heredity, environment, mental health, hormones, extreme beliefs or an accumulation of negative background influences.

In most cases human beings are a product of the age and times in which they live. What is more, repeating the same life and set of circumstances, they would most likely make the same decisions and mistakes again.

At your own funeral & afterwards

Everyone in spirit has the choice to go as an onlooker to their own funeral where they have one. This is in order to hear what is said and see who is there and how they have affected the lives of, and shared experiences with, different people in the congregation.

Your funeral is your first interaction from the other side with humans, their memories and emotions and as such can be quite a shock. For the first time you are able to see what people genuinely think of you, which can be very thought-provoking. As human beings we commonly make the mistake of believing that everyone holds the same opinion of us as we do ourselves, whereas in reality people are individuals with many differing attitudes.

You quickly feel the love of those among the congregation who show it towards you and recognise who is attending more out of a sense of respect or duty because your paths crossed in life. Nevertheless everyone in the congregation has memories personal to them.

The departed can then replay their own memory of the occasion, as with any other memory stored as an energy, like a videotape whenever they choose to in the future. They can dispassionately re-read the personal thoughts and feelings of each person present regarding him or her, positive and negative, whereas from a physical, human point-of-view the sum total of that emotion would be impossible to take in and endure.

Spirits come around their loved ones

In the greater scheme of things, spirit interaction with loved ones in the physical world is the exception rather than the rule. Most spirits have no connection with any relatives or friends currently living on the earth plane and therefore no particular interest in continually visiting it. In time many bloodlines simply die out in any case, and then there may be no one left in the physical world to receive or comprehend messages from family members in spirit who come through to a medium.

However, spirits who wish to can be around relatives and friends, express their love for them and try to help them through human existence's many ordeals and afflictions, whether life-threatening or not.

Spirits can choose to come around you "from time to time" but not "all the time". They may watch and observe how their family or friends are doing things differently to what they did. They themselves can learn from this, but also see what their nearest and dearest need to learn. Yet their life on earth may have been little more than a blip to them in their spiritual life.

A female acquaintance of mine in a village on the north-west Wales coast in Gwynedd has been pleased to witness complete materialisations of her late husband as well as of my wife. That has been at moments when her vibration and energy have exactly synchronised with those of their spirits.

More commonly, spirits may come through just once to greet, and bring love around, their family and close friends still on earth, showing how close they are to them in their daily lives.

Whether conveyed via an evidential medium or direct, their typical messages of reassurance and advice will be in terms such as:

- "Don't worry, I'm perfectly OK now."
- "It's never goodbye, I am always around you."

- “I have met up with our other family members in spirit and am making good progress here.”
- “In my life on earth, I never told people enough that I loved them. So make sure that you share your own love.”
- “Many thanks for all the time and effort that you (and others) spent caring for me, but now you must concentrate on yourself instead. Have the best life that you can!”
- “From now on, be the true You and not what others want you to be.”
- “Life is for living! Get on with your life, enjoy it and stay close to your principles.”

Chapter 6

SOUL PROGRESSION VIA THE LEARNING OF LESSONS

Different levels of vibration or understanding

How good, selfless, charitable, compassionate and helpful – i.e. "spiritual" but not necessarily "spiritualist" – you have been in life towards other evolved living beings helps to determine the "vibration level" or "level of understanding and enlightenment" to which you will go initially in the spirit world, where there are innumerable levels or stages.

As regards acting in a spiritual manner on earth, would you "pass by on the other side" or show compassion and charity and altruistically help a fellow human being in trouble, donate to the rough sleeper in your town centre or intervene to prevent an act of animal cruelty?

It is important to grasp that we are not talking about "levels", higher and lower, in any competitive or judgemental human, physical sense. As explained in Chapter 2, the spirit world is neither competitive nor judgemental in any way.

The faster the vibration, the lighter the energy

To help our understanding, different vibration levels may be better expressed as different "dimensions" – a box within a box within a box within a box, or a balloon within a balloon within a balloon within a balloon, and so on ad infinitum because energy is infinite.

Using this analogy, denser and less developed or enlightened energies will reside in one of the smaller boxes or balloons inside, with the possibility of spirits gradually progressing, as they accumulate experience, to the outer boxes or balloons. The latter are characterised by faster and finer vibrations and populated by higher spirits possessing a greater degree of understanding and experience and therefore a more enlightened consciousness.

Put succinctly, the faster the vibration, the lighter the energy. In contrast, our own environment is characterised by slow vibrations and dense energy: very different to the parallel spirit world around us, we have flesh-and-blood bodies and brick walls.

My paternal grandfather in spirit Alfred Henry Haines recently likened the possible extremes of vibrations within the spirit world to the contrast between a penlight and a stadium arc light! He has piggybacked in on my father's energy several times to give details of his life, as described below.

Photographed here in his 40s, my paternal grandfather AH (Alfred Henry) Haines, who lived for 70 years from 28th May 1851 to 2nd February 1922. My father Richard was the youngest of his and his sharp-tempered, tough-minded wife Mary Ann's seven children. Before World War 1 Alfred Henry had won trophies for bowls, when he played in long cream trousers and a dark blazer, and was, remarkably, ambidextrous – adept at bowling with either hand. He was an accomplished billiards player too in private men's clubs, well able to hold the cue with either hand. There he would smoke cigars and strong cigarettes in the company of business colleagues. He was also a strict timekeeper and disciplinarian, expecting his meal to be ready on the table at a certain time each day when he got home.

Alfred Henry was the surviving founder and director of the family engineering business WH & AH Haines of Fazeley Street in the centre of Birmingham, his brother, the engineering designer WH (William Howard) having died prematurely in 1897. Initially they designed and manufactured wheeled concrete mixers, brick breakers and similar mechanical plant for civil engineering and construction work. Then, between the World Wars, Alfred Henry's successors sold off the patents for their old machines and, moving away from manufacturing, began buying in the latest plant including excavators, pumps and compressors to hire out. An astute businessman and accountant, Alfred Henry's enduring legacy was the major role which his company's capital equipment played in the reconstruction of roads, bridges and buildings after the bombing of the Midlands in World War 2.

If we return to the metaphor of levels, it is possible to lower your vibration to visit a lower level, but not possible to readjust to visit a higher one than that to which you have been initially allocated.

Memories & mind pictures

A spirit entity can revisit any experiences and places from the memory banks of its own persona. It can then describe them exactly to a medium by lowering its vibration to synchronise with that of the medium. That mind picture is exactly as we humans would see it. But using the mind is a two-way process, so that spirit can equally use memories and mental images retained by the medium of his or her own experiences.

In complete contrast, when a spirit visits a location independently in the here-and-now, in real time, it raises its vibration to sense it, from a spirit perspective, as a glowing energy form with bright colours. It is not wholly dissimilar to aura imagery, which we consider later on, in Chapter 12.

Visualisation from wartime memory links

Memory is stored as an energy in the consciousness of loved ones who choose to come through. At 7:30pm on 25th April 2021, during a socially distanced, Sunday evening, Christian Spiritualist service which I attended at the Mereside community centre in Shrewsbury as research for this book, astonishingly an active image of Sir Winston Churchill materialised. It was projected as clear as day simultaneously to platform medium Geoff Morris from Worcester and to the event bookings secretary, also an accomplished medium.

With a broad smile, Winston Churchill was wearing his trademark brimmed Homburg hat and thick overcoat for going out and was smoking one of his large Havana cigars: the smoke could be smelt in the air of the community hall. This universally recognisable manifestation of Winston had come in completely unexpectedly on a memory link from the wartime memories of my mother and father, who came through one after the other, just after he had appeared.

Different spirits are endowed with different strengths, and Winston is now a particularly strong spirit energy, possibly because his character was so formidable and forceful in his last life on the physical plane which ended in January 1965 at the age of 90.

His spirit, which could only be in one place at any one time, had apparently decided to assist our discussion on the value of journalistic research in the context of war reporting, which he had done himself in South Africa in 1899 during the second Boer War. It was an extraordinary experience for everyone present.

Another very strong spirit who has visualised wartime memory links to mediums is an uncle by marriage on my father's side of the family, naval officer Fred Hammond. He is pictured below on his wedding day during shore leave from WW1, when he married my aunt Edith in a modest ceremony at Sedgley, Staffordshire.

She was 19 and he was in his late 20s. As a married navy couple, they later lived in a small house overlooking the sea at Portsmouth.

Shortly after the major naval Battle of Jutland off Denmark in 1916, my uncle Fred Hammond was in command of an armed merchant cruiser – converted for use by the Royal Navy and yet unarmoured and ill-equipped – which was torpedoed amidships by a U-boat of Kaiser Wilhelm II's Imperial German Navy. The severely damaged vessel did not in fact sink but was towed into harbour in Denmark, a neutral nation in World War 1, where it was not repaired but broken up by order of the authorities. Captain Fred Hammond and the survivors from his crew of 150 young men were repatriated to England.

During WW2 and including Dunkirk and D-Day, Fred, a very strong character in keeping with his rank, was in charge of an encrypted radio communications and cipher analysis establishment for the armed forces by Ilfracombe seafront in Devon, visited on several occasions by Air Chief Marshal Lord Hugh Dowding, amongst other notables.

This secret unit for coding and decoding messages was known as HMS Odyssey, a massive Victorian edifice rebuilt in recent times as Wetherspoon's Admiral Collingwood. The wartime operation was staffed by the Women's Royal Naval Service, the WRNS re-established in 1939. Uncle Fred did not pass away until the end of 1953, leaving his widow Edith and their only son Robert at the family home of 52 Manor Road, Solihull, Warwickshire, England. Edith passed in 1989 in her 90s at a care home at Malvern.

Sensing vibrational energies

All physical things, animate and inanimate, movement, sounds and colours are endowed with energy that vibrates. In line with this, operating as they do on a vibrational level, spirits know absolutely what we are saying and yet do not physically hear it with ears.

The more developed you become in the spirit world and the more you learn about your new life, the finer your vibration becomes as a spirit being. Therefore the further away you get from the earth plane in vibration terms, in the spiritual level of your mind. The more successful your journey or continuum is, and as you achieve more, the lighter and brighter you get.

This relates to "the evolution of the spirit and of energy to a higher plane", and not an evolution of the mind per se. Another determinant can be the previous lives which a spirit has led and how much he or she has learned along the way, also from other spirits and from observing human activity.

Life is a school for learning from experiences

The greater appreciation you have of spirituality on the earth plane and in the spirit world, and the more you learn about it and put it into practice, the greater your progression can be towards a higher vibration level or spiritual sphere, where you will be around higher energies. Emotion and thought are of course forms of vibration and energy.

But even greater progression may be achieved by a soul gaining enlightenment from experiences in previous lives on the earth plane – we take different journeys to learn different things. The main purpose of having a physical existence is that we learn lessons from it: life is basically a school for acquiring wisdom.

There is always more to pursue: the process of developing and improving learning is never at an end. Your soul can never know everything there is to know, however many lives it may decide to undertake.

Everyone we meet on our journey through a life can teach us a lesson in some way. We can learn especially from the "hard knocks" of a tough and miserable life and need not necessarily lead a so-called "spiritual" or godly life here to gain advancement.

An "evolution of the clarity of the individual's mind" changes the frequency of the spirit's mind to a faster and finer vibration. The speed of vibration at which spirits exist increases as they become more enlightened and "progress up the ladder", and spirit guides (Chapter 16) are examples of very high-speed vibration.

Moving up to faster & finer vibrations in the spirit world

As discussed in Chapter 3, vibrational energy flows from all living beings, inanimate objects, colours, movement, sounds and so forth in our environment.

Albeit an inexact comparison, but when we ourselves think of vibration, we may contrast the workings of our vocal cords or a tuning fork with the reed in a woodwind instrument or harmonica or the cone-shaped diaphragm of a loudspeaker. Or we might compare the elevated wingbeat frequency of the hummingbird (up to 52 times a second) or a honeybee or fruitfly (over 200 times a second) with birds and insects which vibrate or oscillate their wings at far lower frequencies. Then a laser beam, for instance, may be described as a light vibration.

Quartz timepieces have dominated the wristwatch, clock and timer markets since the 1980s. The precise oscillation of quartz crystals means that timepieces based on them are far more accurate than the best mechanical clocks and watches can ever be.

Vibrational energy is the core element of the spirit world too and has an infinite number of frequency levels. So, bonded by love, family members (or the family unit bonded by love) may prefer to stay together in the same space on a slower vibration or frequency level, rather than the more evolved or ambitious souls among them working their way up in the hierarchy to a higher and finer vibration.

Nevertheless even that would be well below the highest, where highly evolved spirits of the greatest intellect and knowledge – let us say Moses, the prophet Elijah, Socrates, Galileo, Einstein, Hawking or Gandhi – may reside (the spirit guide Edward's words, not mine!). There again, it may be uncomfortable, or not resonate well, for more evolved souls of faster and finer frequency to draw close to the earth plane because of its coarseness as an energy.

Allowing memories of addictions to fade away

The earth plane is characterised by a far slower and heavier vibration. So, as the physical part of your spirit moves up and away from earthly constraints and breaks those shackles upon transition, then your vibration will become faster and finer as a spiritual being.

Shackles may include say emotional and mental cravings for alcohol, nicotine, narcotics or bodily pleasures or obsessive behaviour patterns. These addictions, obsessions and neuroses perish with your mind and body when you migrate to the spirit world. Purely thoughts and memories of them remain, since the soul or spirit has no requirement for anything of a physical nature.

The vibrational energy associated with physical pleasures such as smoking cigarettes or taking drugs is now only a memory and yet may still resonate within the consciousness when that moves on with the spirit from the incarnate to the discarnate state. Memories are stored in the consciousness, and you need to allow the memories of such mental addictions to gradually fade away, as they will, so that they do not have an effect on you as you move forward as a spirit being.

The continuous interaction of mind, body & spirit

Goodness, self-sacrifice and the trait of love for each other are all contained within our soul during its stay in the physical world. And, as we know, the soul – our inner conscience selflessly seeking to help others with community spirit, compassion and generosity in the sharing of love and resources – is eternal and will live on when the brain and body perish and rot.

The soul or spirit within the physical form, being composed of pure energy, cannot be damaged. It simply moves on, strengthened by all the experiences and learning which it has accumulated from that particular human life. Accordingly it can decide to achieve progression by living different lives at different times.

Our mind, body and spirit interact with each other continuously. Similarly to our need for food and drink – which the soul itself does not need to survive, egotism and addictions can take control of our mind and body.

A degree of egotism and strength of personality will always be necessary for us to survive in the culture and surroundings of a competitive world. However, in metaphorical terms, extreme egotism, greed, cravings and obsessive, all-consuming beliefs cause the internal soul or spirit, the higher self, to shrink in size in comparison to mind and body, like a balloon deflating, and to exert less influence. The body's hunger for a particular substance, possibly culminating in substance abuse, overpowers the mind, the brain, which then wants to keep the body satisfied.

Differences in drugs which affect the mind

Addictions can make it harder for the soul to work with and communicate with the person's mind – via his or her conscience which should distinguish right from wrong, good from bad – and to bring mind, body and spirit together, as three equal parts in equilibrium as they should be. Given the chance, the soul would overcome the bad aspects of life that arise from the dominant human ego, ruthless competitiveness and the desire for money, profit, influence and power to the detriment of others.

A craving or addiction often arises in the first place because of something absent from your physical life, for example love and affection, and so the lesson to be learned on that particular journey is how to cope with what is missing from your life.

Relaxants as against painkillers

The use of prescription drugs such as morphine and codeine which deaden pain by numbing signals from the brain, or sedatives treating mental health, will also lessen the chance of successful spirit communication.

But painkillers numbing brain activity are quite different to medications which allow mind and body to let go and relax with euphoric effects, such as nitrous oxide (aka laughing gas). If you are not in pain, it does not mean that you are relaxed.

In addition, the mind-altering, often habit-forming drugs in vogue in 1960s hippie counterculture, like cannabis, LSD and psilocybin ("magic mushrooms") act principally as a psychedelic relaxant for mind and body. They reduce stress and create an euphoric mood that can, potentially at least, open up the mind – the brain in action – to spiritual experiences.

The Mayhew & Huxley experiments with mescaline

The British Member of Parliament Christopher Mayhew described the experience in a controlled experiment filmed for the BBC Panorama programme in December 1955, when he ingested 400mg of a cactus-based alkaloid hallucinogen called mescaline.

He reported: "I am not so conscious of moving myself in space. But I am extremely conscious of moving in time, of things having no succession, and of there being no absolute time, no absolute space. It is simply what we impose on the outside world." The statement ties in very much with Dr Robert Lanza's theory of biocentrism as discussed in Chapter 3.

View this YouTube clip showing the Mayhew experiment:
https://youtu.be/Hd4rgyZzseY

Just prior to this was "The Doors of Perception", a book by the avant-garde English writer and philosopher Aldous Huxley. Published in 1954, it elaborates on his psychedelic experience also under the influence of mescaline in May 1953.

In suppressing the common mind and human ego, the drug induced an altered mental state in which out-of-body experiences similar to Mayhew's became possible for Huxley too. The pioneering psychiatrist and researcher Humphry Osmond, who originally coined the term "psychedelic", supervised the experiment for both Huxley and Mayhew.

There are echoes here too of ayahuasca, a brew made from leaves, seeds and bark and used for a thousand years as a traditional spiritual medicine and an aid to spiritual practice in ceremonies among the indigenous peoples of the Amazon basin.

Arguably not affecting the chemical composition of the brain in the same way as addictive and potentially dangerous hard, man-made and even prescription drugs, psychedelics can only become ingrained as a habit and should not be accompanied by withdrawal symptoms. Chemical receptors in the brain come to accept the new substance in the bloodstream. That is much like obsessively eating chocolate, engaging in a particular pastime, sport or fetish, or undertaking any illogical impulsive or repetitive behaviour.

Earning progression by helping traumatised souls

Progression is a question of to what extent you learn your lessons and gain enlightenment, not necessarily the length of earthly time you may have been in spirit. Initially the soul goes to the vibration level at which that soul has earned the right to exist. There is no physical barrier or wall between different levels or planes, differentiated merely by their vibration.

For example, my late mother Gwen as a conservationist and environmentalist was a champion of / campaigner for birds and animals on earth (a spiritual quality) and has chosen to do this for their souls in the spirit world, assisting her progression to a higher level of understanding and enlightenment.

At the same time, other spirits choose to reassure and support unwanted, loveless and maltreated children entering the spirit world, patiently drawing them out and gaining their confidence.

The souls of such distressed children may develop and evolve with a greater love and understanding from spirits around them than they may ever have experienced on the earth plane. Thus gaining reassurance, the children's souls further brighten as they are introduced to the young personae of other spirits. A child figure in spirit will know another child better than any adult.

Working with the spirits of transitioned animals

My mother has told us that the spirits of birds, which she recognises as an ornithologist, are limited to seven lives as a bird on the physical plane. That is before returning permanently to their home in the spirit world, or alternatively choosing a different animal for reincarnation.

In an informal chat using Skype on 3rd April 2021 she was viewed alongside me holding a colourful parrot. Amazingly it was in fact the spirit incarnation of the original parrot which she had kept in her childhood after the First World War and which had now used up its seven physical lives. She added that the animal species held in highest regard in the spirit world was incidentally the white dove, as the worldwide symbol of peace, love and peace movements since Biblical times.

As far as my mother is concerned, it was always part of her journey or pathway to be an animal lover. On earth she regarded all life, animal or human, as equally precious and believed that the degree of civilisation of any nation, or the godliness of any religion, is measured by how its people treat animals, being unable to speak for themselves.

The moral teaching of Gandhi on animals

Accordingly my mother agreed wholeheartedly with the oft-quoted words of the social reformer and moral teacher Mahatma Gandhi, echoing his spiritual convictions: "The greatness of a nation and its moral progress can be judged by the way its animals are treated."

In spirit she has worked, as a member of a team, with the spirits of transitioned animals burdened with memories, although not feelings, of their pain and suffering on earth, caused for instance by deliberate human cruelty or bloodsports killing for pleasure purposes only, in short the worst abuses of man's power over their fellow creatures.

My mother Gwen Haines, 1915-2001

Equally, she has put thoughts into the minds of humans with whom she can interact to care better for the animals under their control and prolong their lives, thus allowing those animals' continued interaction with the souls of others on earth.

Gaining enlightenment from other spirits around, helping others through healing – or through teaching new entrants to the spirit world – are further skillsets which assist progression up the ladder.

Many recent newcomers arriving confused or psychologically damaged (such as suicide or accident victims) need tutoring, support and a metaphorical "arm around the shoulder". Spirit energy will blend with that of a suicide or accident victim ("becoming one" as discussed earlier), in order to help that troubled individual to find emotional peace, stability and tranquillity and move on with their journey in the company of their loved ones already in spirit.

My father Richard (Dick) Haines (1907-1985), pictured in February 1944 as a Lance Corporal in the Derbyshire Yeomanry. He had driven vital water supply trucks for General Montgomery's Eighth Army in the baking heat at the decisive second battle of El Alamein in Egypt, during October and November 1942. Then he served in Holland at Nijmegen and Arnhem along the River Rhein following the D-Day invasion by the Allies in June 1944. He married Gwen in Sheldon, Birmingham, on 1st May 1947. As she was, he was extremely compassionate and a genuine friend of animals.

Thereby traumatised souls learn to review their human life and to accept how their demise came about or why they did what they did, and how they will now be embarking upon a new phase of their life in the spirit world.

Changing for the better

In contrast to the positivity of spirituality, a deep-seated anger, aggression, judgemental or bitter attitude towards life and people, an unbridled ego, or hardline religious beliefs of whatever persuasion, would hold you back in spirit. They would hamper the learning of lessons and your progression up the spiritual tree, the evolution of your soul. You could not harm anyone but yourself through anger in the realm of spirit.

In the spirit dimension there is no place on a higher vibration level for, let us say, murderers who loved violence and intended it, or those who on earth have exhibited extreme greed or depravity: the question of premeditated intent is a significant factor here.

But placement on a certain level is never permanent, and salvation is possible for every soul, should they wish to change their ways, embrace personal enlightenment and develop their potential for improvement.

We wake up to how we have been, how we have acted, and want to change for the better. In gospel terms, we all need to be honest, acknowledge our sins and repent of them!

Enemies are no longer enemies

Even the worst will grow into feeling compassion, love and consideration for others. The truth – frequently attributed to Gandhi – sinks in that "an eye for an eye will only make the whole world blind".

Extreme enemies based on their polarised views on earth, such as Nazis and Jews, Romanovs and Bolsheviks, Hindus and Muslims, Sikhs and Muslims, Sunnis and Shiites, or Hutus and Tutsis, do get to renounce their hatreds, move on and love each other in the spirit world. The lion will truly lie down with the lamb. Then they have only memories of their former enmities, because Love – with a capital "L" – is literally the only show in town.

Furthermore, the greater the progression they make, the more easily spirits can communicate with those left behind on the earth plane.

In one fascinating platform demonstration of his evidential mediumship, Robin received communication for a woman in the audience from both of her previous husbands, coming in together. In the spirit world these bitter rivals no longer had any ill feeling towards each other and wished to step forward together to express equal affection and best wishes for her wellbeing. In spirit, love is literally the only emotion.

Chapter 7

COMMUNICATING WITH SPIRIT

Temporary soul groups of personae

A soul group or spirit family – whether composed of relatives by bloodline or marriage, friends or other significant contacts from past lives – is a joint consciousness coming together from different vibration levels which can communicate internally with its members. But, interestingly, "best friends" in the physical world do not necessarily retain that close relationship spirit-to-spirit.

The soul group is marshalled by the spirit world and is drawn not particularly from just the last physical life. Different soul groups will partially overlap like Olympic rings or circles, so that an individual spirit can belong to different groups. One group can include hundreds of spirits.

Remember that spirits are also people. They assemble temporarily as a group of personae from different vibrations for a defined purpose – typically to enrich each other's existences or to let themselves be known to a medium (projecting their images onto his or her mind) in order to assist communication with the medium as an interlocutor.

They also gather in anticipation of welcoming a loved one home, a "meet-and-greet" when a transition is on the cards, or to boost the morale of individuals or otherwise spur them to carry on in their physical life when they are feeling low. Spirits can bring forward the more assertive, resilient or tenacious aspects of their previous human personality, as may be needed by the recipient to strengthen his or her resolve in current difficult situations.

For my sittings with mediums, my own relatives come together like a family reunion as a soul group, building up a stronger energy when combined. The number of personae attending from that last, most recognisable life varies from sitting to sitting and depends upon what information they want to bring forward. What do they wish to tell us?

At other times, not being bound together physically, they go their own ways to "do their own thing". Otherwise individual spirits may pop in and out to see how people they knew or loved are getting on with their physical lives, whoever or whatever may interest those spirits.

A communicator chosen by the soul group

As far as communication is concerned, an individual will step forward as the chosen representative or ambassador of the soul group for that occasion, to lend deeper and wider experience and assist the dialogue with the medium. Meanwhile the joint energy of the group in the background helps to power this communication from spirit.

The right person comes through for the right reason at the time. It could be someone whom you met once in your life fleetingly for five minutes, but who, unbeknown to you at the time, touched you on a soul level. It is not necessarily whom you think you want, but whose advice you need to help your current situation on earth. Thereby you can have access within the joint consciousness of the soul group to specialist professional minds such as engineers, technicians, teachers, medics, chefs, artists and craftsmen.

Such a group, loosely composed of like-minded personae with common emotional connections and whose lives have crossed on the earth plane, can be regarded as being analogous to a football team on earth. Accordingly, after the game (the dialogue), they will disperse and go their separate ways, to move on with their personal soul progression.

Synchronicity that enables communication

By completely relaxing, slowing our thinking down and quietening our minds through deep meditation, we can open up our awareness and attune to the higher vibration at which spirits around us exist. Thereby we can communicate with them as personae, exchanging thoughts, mind images, emotions and sensations. The busy brain activity of our conscious mind must take a back seat and not get in the way.

Apart from quietening our minds, we need to raise our vibration to become aware of the spirits around us, whilst they need to lower theirs to a denser, heavier energy to communicate with us. The synchronicity of vibrations one with the other, as well as the similarity of the two energies involved, are key factors in making a better connection for that communication to work. Then a slightly higher vibration, with a perceptible change of energy, from the same spirit can provide a different quality or type of information, based upon higher intellect.

But bear in mind that not all spirits wish, nor indeed have the skills, to communicate with us. We have to realise that it is very much their choice and not ours.

They absolutely live around us on earth and in our space but on a different vibration. The process of synchronisation may be likened to tuning a radio until you find the desired frequency.

Cerebral activity & comatose states

The irony is that paraplegics and other such seriously disabled people with limited faculties can have extrasensory perception and awareness much greater than ours and may sense the presence of spirit far better than the able-bodied. Their cerebral activity and thought patterns are all limited by their condition – since they cannot use many of our senses, activate their limbs, etc – with the result that their spirit-to-spirit communication becomes far more developed, focussed and intense.

Their remaining senses "work overtime" to compensate for the non-functioning ones. Similarly, a comatose state induced by anaesthetic or analgesic drug in a hospital, ambulance or other nursing environment heightens people's awareness of what is going on around them.

How often do responsible nurses and carers warn bedside visitors that patients made drowsy with pain-killing drugs, or in an induced coma, deadening some of their senses, can "hear everything that is said in the room"? The spirit of the patient certainly picks up everything going on around the bed and can report this in detail after transition, as did my wife's late aunt during my sittings with Robin Clayton.

Chapter 8

THE ART OF MEDIUMSHIP

The role of mental mediums

A medium is basically a person who has the ability to see, hear or otherwise sense beings in the parallel spirit universe and who can convey messages from them to our physical world.

The evidential or mental medium is a gifted individual able to read, and communicate telepathically with, the consciousness of a transitioned spirit – or indeed a spirit still within a body (as living spirit to living spirit) – acting as a channel or conduit for messages similar to a telephone line.

In uncommon examples of visualisation mediumship – often an inherited gift where all spirits in the vicinity are visible to the medium – spirits in the medium's field of vision in the course of a message will purposely appear in ages and guises most familiar to the audience member or sitter.

Understandably, extreme cases of "clairvoyance" or "clear seeing" can at times be more of a curse than a gift, so that then the medium involved needs to be skilled and disciplined in "shutting down" his or her natural awareness and ordering invasive spirits to desist and depart!

Robin Clayton, a working British psychic medium who has been providing evidence since 2008 of our survival after death

The gifts of spirit-to-spirit communication and clairvoyance (seeing spirit) are not exclusive to practising mediums. As an example, Mhine, an expatriot Filipina married to an Englishman and living in Staffordshire, UK, freely helps and supports friends in need and her many spirit contacts by using her natural communication skills, seen as her mission in life. This is all led by her maternal grandmother as not only her primary spirit guide, but also her personal gatekeeper, to authorise or deny access to Mhine by the strongest and most demanding spirits.

Indeed Mhine acquired her highly advanced skills in clairvoyance and healing from this late grandmother Demitheria Gutiérrez, a staunch Roman Catholic. Demitheria lived close to and donated land to a large church shrine at Manaoag in Pangasinan province, western Luzon, Philippines, which dates back three centuries and is now designated by Rome as a minor basilica.

With the intellect of spirit, she had alerted Mhine no less than two years before, in three separate dreams, that a stranger of my description and background would appear by chance in her life needing her assistance and support. As her guide, Demitheria similarly flags up in Mhine's dreams every person who is going to need her future psychological help.

If you can synchronise your consciousness with that of spirits to the extent that you enjoy their complete trust, then any of the skillsets I describe later, such as clairvoyance, precognition, psychography (automatic writing) and psychometry (reading the history of objects), can be made available to you, which is the case with Mhine. As well as her inherited, most rare gift of being able to see spirit all the time, she can close her eyes and get glimpses into the future, the precognition of events as described in Chapter 3. Later in the current Chapter, I explain how automatic writing or psychography works via an intermediary spirit, and Mhine is now writing such pages automatically from different personalities in the spirit world with different handwriting styles.

In other respects, Mhine's perception of spirit is formed by her own acquired belief system, and the spirit world can always choose to accommodate, or go along with, your particular belief system and expectations in cases where that will smooth the way for your spiritual development and advancement.

Hence, in the sky above her, she claims to observe – on a dark and low vibrational level of the spirit realm close to our physical world – a mass of rootless souls who have neither accepted their new reality nor repented of their sins on earth. Despite having been met on their transition by past relatives and friends with the essence of love, they are still hesitant about taking the next step and moving on into the light. Some spirits in this galaxy of people stay still, others whizz past at high speed or proceed more slowly, going in whichever direction they wish.

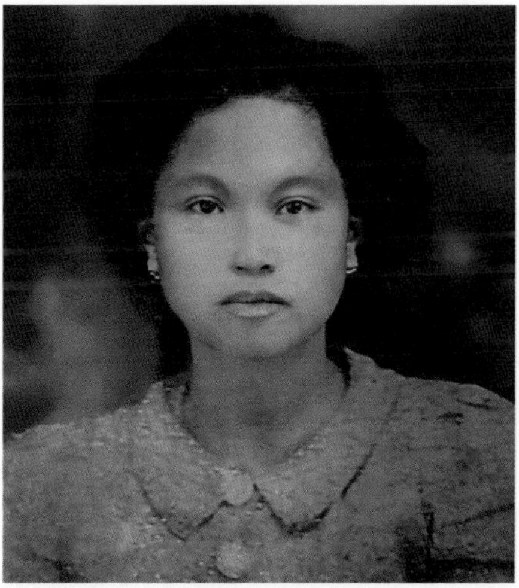

Demitheria Gutiérrez photographed in the Philippines in her 40s

Whilst spirits perceive other spirits as pure energy, to Mhine half of those in the host appear in their physical form with names and faces, half as balls of energy. She hears how they meet and talk to one another, asking basic questions such as: "What is your name?", "Do you miss your family?", "Where did you live?", "What work did you do?", "How did you die?" – in English or whatever terrestrial language is common to both.

Mhine also suggests that the spirits of past family members in the multitude might not recognise each other without linking in with their common bloodline remaining on the earth plane, of whatever generation. Memory links need to be re-established, and families, in pursuing their own busy earthly lives, can simply forget their loved ones who have passed to spirit.

The evidential medium has limited terms of reference, having been programmed to provide proof from a spirit's last life strongest in present memory and not to substantiate lives previous to that. Accordingly, controlling the conversation with intellect far superior to ours, spirit will stick to that way of working with the medium, their shared purposes being to relieve our pain in losing loved ones and to prove the existence of spirit.

There are no issues with foreign languages because communication with the medium is just by thought, mind-to-mind, around the world. The "power of thought", a science in itself, brings the message forward to the medium. So this is universal, and there is no language barrier.

Another characteristic of evidential communications is that they do not specify dates and times in our past, present or future, simply because, as described back in Chapter 1, the spirit world is a world without time. Therefore those receiving a message may need to look for its relevance to their lives over a far greater timescale than they expect, or it may even refer to their future and not have happened yet.

The physicality of the medium can intrude

Fundamentally, the content and flow of the conversation are governed by the spirit communicator, and the medium is purely and simply the mouthpiece.

During this process of exclusively spirit-to-spirit communication, the medium needs to stop his or her common physical mind coming into play, except insofar as he or she needs to pass on messages to other humans present. Above and beyond the medium's spirit which gets the contact, the physicality of the medium can come into play and interfere with the connection made.

The medium may perhaps be in physical or emotional pain or discomfort. Or intense emotions can often be introduced by the spirit communicator, and if, as a result, the medium gets too carried along by them, then the link to spirit is in danger of being lost.

Conditions affecting the quality of communication

There has to be a balance of numerous variables to achieve effective spirit-to-spirit contact, blending and interaction for communication purposes. The essential starting-point has to be how clear the medium's mind is physically to accept the message.

Thereafter the circumstances have to be more or less right, if not spot-on. Accordingly, factors will range from the synchronicity of vibrations and similarity of energies (as discussed above), to the consciousness and state-of-mind of the medium and the persona, aims and skill level of the spirit communicator.

The medium's energy blends with the energy of the spirit who decides to come through, or to step forward as the spokesperson for a group of spirits. Being part of the group consciousness, non-participating spirits in the background are "in on the conversation" and know fully what is being discussed.

Remote viewing across the miles

The medium is able to view, as it were through the spirit's eyes, visual memories projected from its immediate past life and, momentarily at least, share the health, senses and sensations of its physical body.

What is more, "remote viewing" through the spirit's eyes – via astral projection of the spirit, independent mind travel as described in Chapter 2 – can walk the medium through faraway buildings, sites and landscapes in real time.

The American physicists Harold E Puthoff and Russell Targ of the Electronics and Bioengineering Laboratory at Stanford Research Institute in California coined this term "remote viewing".

They conducted related experiments from 1972 onwards, making a major contribution to the US Federal Government's Stargate Project based at Fort Meade in Maryland. This ran up to 1995 for the purpose of investigating the potential employment of psychic abilities in military tactics, to see what was happening behind enemy lines.

Messages from spirit have a specific purpose

Allowing the medium to feel its energy, a spirit always steps forward for a definite purpose – usually to advise, support, comfort or warn a relative or friend of theirs on the earth plane. In all communications spirit will be 100% truthful, having no reason to tell lies about facts, since falsehoods are a purely human trait.

Nevertheless spirit in its wisdom is fully aware of how far it can go with passing on information to the physical world. Thus it may at times shy away from answering a question because of the serious impact on an individual of hearing an unpalatable truth, for example news of a life-threatening medical condition or an imminent decease.

At a platform demonstration, messages of comfort and support tend to come through for the audience members who most need them at that particular time. In a word, the strength of purpose of a message determines its place in the queue.

Takeaway messages from spirit

There are also "takeaway messages" from spirit, intentionally for the recipient to pass on later to a known, absent third party, possibly a sceptic who would never have the chance of, nor think of, seeing a medium work.

A takeaway message may be the only way in which spirits can communicate what they have to say to the intended receiver. Unlike a regular message, its accuracy cannot be substantiated there and then at the venue.

The medium can just as easily communicate with the spirit of someone in a permanent vegetative state or coma who is non-verbal and non-responsive. Indeed, my friend Robin has successfully communicated with the spirit of such a person in a coma in hospital. The spirit remains in the body until the very last flickerings of life have gone and physical death has taken place.

Simultaneous communication with the same spirit

Interestingly, two or three mediums, with naturally varying minds, personalities and life experiences, can work alongside each other in a double or even triple link. They will communicate simultaneously in this way with the consciousness of the same spirit in order to bring forward different aspects of that spirit's previous physical personality, appearance and life on the earth plane.

By nature a female medium is likely to pick up on different but complementary traits of character than a male medium who is present, to arrive as it were at a balance of yin and yang from Chinese philosophy.

What is more, because of ingrained cultural differences between the sexes, there are bound to be subjects which either a male or a female spirit consciousness would feel uncomfortable discussing with a medium of the opposite gender.

Different mediums, different messages

As we are saying, so many variables come into the equation, since different mediums will vary in terms of how their mind works (and how that links in with spirit), their personality, background and experience, and the flexibility they show in sensing, cooperating with and communicating with spirit. Mediums able to adapt to different ways of working tend to be compatible with a greater range of spirits and accordingly encourage more to step forward.

Messages can be of different depths for different recipients. Some mediums are accustomed to passing on from spirit very accurate messages quoting ages, relationships, dates and even names and addresses, whilst others will describe the deceased person's character, feelings and appearance without specifying names and dates. A medium whose characteristic is to hardly use the names of people and places in daily life and conversation will not tend to work with names from the platform!

A medium can obtain accurate messages from the afterlife, including "nuggets" of unique evidence, to convey to individual sitters, to a member of an assembled audience or to a person on the other side of the world – distance is no barrier to mediumship.

The power of the human voice in response raises the energy and so helps with the link to spirit. The only three, loud and clear, responses that a mental medium requests from the audience member or sitter to the information conveyed from the spirit world are: "Yes", "No" or "I don't know".

That is because any further background fed into the medium's mind would pre-empt and get confused with the evidence that spirit is attempting to deliver via the same route. Indeed there are a variety of practical reasons why the three-way dialogue should always start with a completely blank canvas.

Sharing messages, memories & deep emotions

The quality, clarity and intelligibility of any message are key. Conversely, spirit needs to provide evidence as corroboration to the medium too.

Mediums are "sensitives" who can come from any civilisation, country or background. In effect they work much like interpreters or translators from one language into another. They share messages, memories and deep emotions.

The personality, vocabulary, life experiences and memories of individual mediums can play a role, and yet they are peripheral to the sum and substance of spirit's communications.

Having said that, spirits are naturally attracted to communicate through mediums who show like-for-like emotional, familial or experiential parallels to their own life stories, because such mediums will speak with greater understanding and empathy. Spirits use the memories of mediums. For instance, the loss of a child or the challenges of relationship issues, violent conduct or drug abuse may be experiences that they share.

Conveying messages as faithfully as possible

On the negative side, although mediums always need a degree of confidence and self-belief, their ego, common mind and lack of experience can diminish the quality of the message and make it difficult for communicators from spirit to achieve what they want to. An inexperienced medium may not be in the right frame of mind.

Mediums should pass on messages faithfully from the departed without embellishment and share their memories, as well as picking up empathetically on their feelings. Nevertheless, to put thought patterns and feelings into words can be very challenging, even if mediums are highly articulate and have a good command of language.

The essence of love lies behind every message. In addition, the experience of conveying messages of love in this way can play havoc with mediums' emotions. The spirit-to-spirit energy will give them an euphoric "high", as to a lesser extent can communication with a lively, humorous spirit.

And yet their task of adequately "passing on love" from spirit communicator to audience member or sitter is really impossible to achieve. That is because love in the spirit world is of an intensity far beyond human experience and comprehension.

At a level recipients can understand

The medium has to exercise personal responsibility and put all those spirit messages and feelings, with accuracy, sensitivity and tact, into a vocabulary and at a level that individual recipients can understand, as well as accept with their ego.

The spirit's personality from his or her physical life comes through to the medium "warts and all", so that bad language for example needs to be censored out of a message before it is delivered! If a spirit was say fast-talking and garrulous in his last human life, then he will be just the same "motormouth" when talking to any medium.

And you have to avoid "opening things up" in messages, thereby exposing an audience member's private and personal details from the platform.

Recipients have to work out the message conveyed via the medium from the spirit communicator, so that it is essentially a three-way process. Content is tailored by spirit, not by the medium, to the intellect and comprehension of receivers at that stage of their knowledge of the spirit world and should not go over their heads. Variables in the whole process include how the medium works with spirit and which of the medium's memories spirit can draw upon.

All of this can at times be very hard to accomplish. Recipients may possess only limited spiritual knowledge, mental capacity and comprehension, or may not believe that spirits even exist. Yet the deeper the understanding that they choose to develop over time, the greater the depth of information spirit will feel able to bring through for them. That has certainly been true in my own case.

How the intelligence of spirit can ease pain of bereavement

Spirit entities know in advance how the information they impart will be received. For example, most of the bereaved who receive messages see their loved ones as retaining human form and faculties and continuing to pursue their favourite earthly pastimes in the spirit environment! However, if that information is quite sufficient to assuage humans' grief, then spirit can consider it as "job done" and recognise that there is no point in enlightening them further and confusing the fond picture they hold in their minds.

And how will a message affect its recipient emotionally and physically in life? It can mean so much. The delivery of any information may be postponed until such time as spirit judges that it will not be too premature and psychologically damaging, or when human support will be more readily available.

In essence, spirit aims to choose the right place at the right time using the right medium for presenting information, so as to make the message the best it can be for the person receiving it.

Adjusting the vibrational level of the brain

Through different meditative exercises and the strengthening of their sensitivity and awareness, evidential mediums develop the ability to attune to the spirit side of life which exists around us, sharing our space. So, having quietened their minds to exclude all surrounding chatter and clutter invading the brain from the five senses, they have the ability to change their brainwaves for spirit operating on a higher vibrational level to come in. The raising of the medium's vibration in this way was historically called "the quickening".

My medium friend Robin communicates on an energetic, so-called "love vibration" with the personae of my past family members spirit-to-spirit, or soul-to-soul, rather than indirectly via a third communicator – a spirit guide operating at a far higher vibration. Robin's inner spirit, inner self, soul if you like, therefore interacts directly with individual transitioned family spirits, in a process of mind-to-mind or energy-to-energy. Like a radar or receiving antenna, he gets a picture in his mind, backed up by verbal and sensory communications from spirit.

Affinity between medium & spirit communicator

Energies need to blend spirit-to-spirit to achieve successful communication. Vibrational levels will always vary from medium to medium, and the family or soul group member with the level corresponding with – or synchronising most closely with – the medium's will often be the one to make the connection, step forward and speak on behalf of the others.

It is entirely the spirit's prerogative whether to step forward or not. The spirit who comes through may easily be a past family member or acquaintance quite different from the one the recipient is expecting to hear from!

Then some spirits are more confident in, skilled in or accustomed to communicating through mediums than others. Thus new entrants to the spirit world lacking in confidence can be nervous or reserved in communicating, whilst talkative spirits show a particular affinity with Robin, who is himself talkative and extrovert. For example, he and my uncle Bill, as described later in this Chapter, share the same dry sense of humour, making the dialogue between them very relaxed and a lot of fun.

Therefore compatibility with the personality of the medium helps energies and communication enormously. Interestingly my wife feels that there is a problem coming through, as spirit communicator for the family, with mediums whose style is excessively brusque and quick-fire.

Energy emissions from modern technology

It is worth mentioning that the increasing amount of man-made energy and electromagnetic interference (EMI) bombarding our brains can interfere not only with our personal energy field but also with the transfer of natural energy vibrations from spirit to, for example, mediums.

The culprits are modern-day electrical and electronic systems and mechanisms – power lines, phone networks, wi-fi, lighting, alarms, widescreen TVs, microwave devices, voice command devices, medical scanners, quartz watches and so forth.

Now, in the international rush to deploy competing, superfast fifth-generation (5G) digital cellular communications networks which use higher frequency radio waves, little or no attention has been paid to the heightened environmental impact of this technology and the energy-emitting local infrastructure that it will demand. There will be no escape from the emissions.

By using higher frequency waves than earlier mobile networks, 5G allows more devices to have access to the Internet at the same time and at faster speeds. These waves travel shorter distances through urban spaces, so that 5G networks require far more transmitter masts – positioned closer to ground level on existing roadside infrastructure – than previous mast systems.

When in close proximity, these modern technologies can restrict the depth of messages received by the medium, although they have no effect at all on the communicators from spirit, who remain invulnerable and indestructible. Mediums ideally need clean vibrational energy, without distortion, with which to work. Such competition between man-made and natural energies was hardly an issue centuries ago!

A form of healing to help the bereaved

The rare skill of mediumship can be considered as a form of healing to help the bereaved to understand and accept their loss and overcome the anguish. Much unwarranted mystique, apprehension and even dread have grown up around mediumship, and yet reality shows that it is a simple and straightforward skill which people can acquire through training and attuning their mind to the requisite higher vibration.

The children or grandchildren of an existing medium seem to be already mentally attuned and thus to have a "head start" in developing the capability, should they choose to take that path. No one has yet explained quite why the bloodline, the line of descent, is so important in this respect.

Nevertheless, although they are accustomed to know when their (say) late mother, father or sibling is around them by his or her energies, evidential mediums cannot easily communicate with such a close relative of their own. Their own mind comes into it too much – they will already be holding in their consciousness an abundance of knowledge and memories of that person. In such a case they cannot readily distinguish between fresh evidence coming in from spirit and their existing store of memories.

The role of tutors in training mediums

Dedicated to meditation, mediums have learned and practised the ability to open up and accept mind pictures and messages from spirits by lowering or clearing their natural busy brain activity through preceding minutes of meditation, linking in with the frequency of spirits.

The process of learning on a spiritual level is conducted through experienced mediums who are also course tutors. The best ones work spirit-to-spirit, and there can be a waiting list of years to be accepted onto top-notch courses for necessarily small groups. In contrast, spiritual workshops and seminars are normally one-off events.

Tutors need to familiarise themselves with the spiritual level of each individual student in their small group, so as to improve a student's skills and move him or her up to a higher level of communication with the spirit world. And not only students but also working mediums should be looking to continually develop or fine-tune their craft in this way.

Sensing the spirits of animals

When they are successfully "in the zone", mediums can feel the presence – as

My wife Pam's first spaniel, a female English springer spaniel called Chi-Chi, on the beach at Sidmouth, Devon, in August 1993. As the most spiritual of her pet dogs over the years, Chi-Chi was the one with whom she had the greatest understanding and closest relationship, spirit-to-spirit with no need for language. Accordingly, when Pam's spirit took her final journey, Chi-Chi's energy was there, alongside every past being she had ever loved, animals and people, to greet and calm her, and make her transition more comfortable.

energy – of the souls not only of people but also of pet animals, such as cats, dogs and horses, and even rabbits, tortoises and cage birds, which in life may have enjoyed a long and close relationship with their human owners.

A medium can for instance tell the approximate age – as with a human in spirit – of a pet by its energy. Nevertheless it is not possible for the medium to communicate psychically with animals' spirits, because their physical mind or brain is configured differently to that of a person.

Yet, within the spirit world, spirit is just spirit, communicating seamlessly with each other by thought, so that whether a previous physical life on earth was as a dog or as a human being is irrelevant.

For example, my wife Pam can communicate, by thought, with the soul energies of her former pet dogs where they are together with her now in the spirit world. But she would have been unable to communicate with them when she was in spirit and they were still living in the physical world. In the latter case they might merely react noticeably to the feeling, the sensation, when her spirit was close to them.

Her present spirit-to-spirit communication with former animals is far easier than with humans because the human brain gets too clogged up with information, whereas animals have fewer thoughts and preoccupations. All that a dog wishes to do is to please its owner, give pure love and get fed, watered, looked after and taken on walks problem-free.

The medium assumes the spirit's persona

The mediumistic communication link becomes a voyage of discovery. The medium assumes the persona of the spirit who comes through. Spirits can let the medium feel their character and health traits and see their physiognomy, build and attire at any particular time in their life.

They can come forward in whatever guise and at whatever age they wish to, although make every effort to appear as a person whom people might recognise. For instance, we might well have great difficulty in identifying an ancestor portrayed as a child!

The date of physical death is a far more significant milestone for a spirit entity to commemorate – and indeed celebrate as a homecoming – than the date of birth, the birthday. From the spirit's perspective, birthdays are of no consequence. Hence the initial mind picture that a medium will often request for reference is of the subject just before their passing.

If spirits so wish, they are able to acquaint the clairsentient medium with the circumstances and give an inkling of the bodily aches, pains or mental disorientation which they had felt in the period prior to their transition.

If, for example, the medium experiences a sudden, temporary difficulty during a demonstration in getting words out, drooling from the corner of the mouth, this would suggest that the spirit communicator is projecting a past life memory of suffering the effects of a stroke.

Short-lived sensing of bodily aches & pains

But the empathetic (clairsentient) medium's physical discomfort is minimised, because spirits preserve and can convey just a brief memory, lasting no more than a few seconds, of those feelings experienced in their physical life, even if the pain had in reality gone on for months or years. The feelings are fed into the medium's mind rather than provided direct by vibrational energy, which could prove detrimental to the medium's body and long-term health.

Spirits, who having no body cannot feel bodily pain, are fully sensitive to a medium's pain threshold and will convey fleetingly only so much to the medium as he or she can bear. As soon as the medium has felt it and revealed it to the audience or sitter, spirits will take it away.

Interestingly, throughout the communication session all pre-existing, personal aches and pains of head and body are overtaken by the new sensations and therefore cease to be felt by the medium.

Conveying memories of tastes & feelings

In fact spirits can momentarily let the medium sense many things, primarily the memories of their emotions, tastes and feelings. That might include, for instance, an aroma of tobacco smoke if they were a smoker, a dryness or acid indigestion reflux in the throat, or a shortness of breath from the underlying heart and lung complaint which may have taken them to the spirit world.

Then a taste in the mouth may be a symptom felt by the medium consistent with an iron deficiency or diabetes, if such health conditions had previously applied to those individuals during their physical existence. A dry throat may indicate the use of oxygen in hospital.

Equally, the memory of a particular wine or fizzy drink can be communicated to the taste buds of the medium. Or the medium can sense the wearing of such things as false teeth, watches, jewellery, flat shoes, platform soles or high heels. So the list of sensory perceptions goes on!

The story of my uncle Bill

In putting across a personal story, the pictures introduced into a medium's mind can be quite astonishing. On the night of 12th December 1971 my uncle Bill Haines (1906-71) was tragically decapitated by the starboard engine of an incoming Britannia Airways Boeing 737 jet carrying 108 holidaymakers and six crew who were returning from Alicante. He had wandered in a mentally confused state across the grass onto Runway 33 of the former Birmingham Elmdon airport.

Bill Haines the footballer and cricketer. Centre forward for the Birmingham County FA representative team against the Scottish Junior FA at Heart of Midlothian FC, Tynecastle Park, Edinburgh, on 26th April 1930. On the right, a player at Solihull Cricket Club in Marsh Lane, Solihull, throughout the 1950s and 1960s.

Now Bill likes to amuse us with his black humour: he often conveys to my medium friend Robin a mind picture of himself with his head tucked neatly under his arm like the fabled ghost of Anne Boleyn! Bill had had an illustrious sporting career, including several games between the Wars for the England amateur football team as centre forward, and yet, much to his amusement, he is best remembered nowadays not for that but for the dramatic manner of his demise.

Amazingly it was as painless as it was instantaneous, and, ironically, any shock and anguish affected not him but rather the multiplicity of people caught up in the incident and its aftermath, as well as their loved ones down the line. And it had the positive effect of persuading the airport authorities to upgrade their perimeter fencing for the next generation!

So up to now uncle Bill has lived seven lives over hundreds of years, four as males in Britain (the first, second, sixth and seventh) and the other three as females in different parts of the world.

His first life was as a humble woodsman with the surname of Richmond, who lived in the medieval village of Clare in south-west Suffolk. Suitable wood was essential for making bows, and bowmanship was a skill required by law for every able Englishman of that era. Richmond was imprisoned for poaching deer from a forest next to where he lived, and he died from disease whilst in prison.

His second male life was as Jonathan Williams (known as Jack), a portly, red-coated town crier in Wandsworth, now south-west London. He married the daughter of the first licensee of the historic Leather Bottle public house in Garratt Lane, still open for business now after 300 years. His strong social conscience drove him to campaign for community amenities including a public park with an open-air swimming pool, public baths and a washhouse for people's clothes.

Bill's first female life was as Gretchen Rolfberg, a member of wealthy Austrian nobility who lived in a castle. She used to dress up in fine clothes and dance olde worlde Viennese waltzes. "Oneupmanship" was the order of the day in the social circle, social standing counted for everything, and mixing was quite limited outside the family. Gretchen had a wasteful brother (killed in a duel fought over money) and a sister for company as she grew up. She bore two children of her own and lived to see her grandchildren. She passed from pneumonia at 87 years of age.

After Gretchen, Bill was Anne-Marie Woods, a poor prostitute's daughter in rural Herefordshire. She succumbed to tuberculosis in the 1800s when only in her later teens.

In complete contrast, his fifth life was as Elisabeth, the wealthy wife of Arthur Wilburn, a cotton plantation owner and vegetable grower in southern Mississippi, the largest cotton producing region of North America. He did employ black slaves to bring in the harvests and yet was well known for treating them with humanity and compassion. Then everything changed when the American Civil War led to the abolition of slavery throughout the United States, with Congress passing the 13th Amendment to the Constitution in 1865.

The life as my uncle, passing at 65 in 1971, was his sixth. In his seventh and last life for now, which was under the name of James William Redgrave (known as William), he succumbed in 2005 to a form of leukaemia at only 9½ years of age. His life ended in an old hospice adjacent to the Birmingham Children's Hospital, and his devoted mother Mary stayed with him the whole time. William had lived with his parents and an elder brother between the Worcestershire villages of Hagley and Fairfield.

He had been treated in the Hospital in the latter stages, alongside other children who were suffering from similar terminal blood disorders and with whom he formed a unique bond of friendship. An older patient in their bay of four at the hospice – a 12-year-old girl who died after him – comforted him and helped him to come to terms with his own dying.

The further lesson that William learned spiritually was how to let go of the people who loved him deeply within his own family. As spirit, he could see the strength of his parents' emotions, feeling the outpourings of their love as well as the pain they were going through.

All of this, in his own words, taught him a deeper appreciation of the meaning of love than did anything in his previous six lives. I will be further discussing the subject of past lives in Chapter 15.

Drawing upon the medium's own knowledge

Spirits will use our own minds in any way they can and work with memories that we have stored over our lifetime. And so, as I described earlier in this Chapter, spirits are naturally attracted to communicate through mediums whose lives show like-for-like correlations with their own life stories and who therefore understand the problems and empathise more.

It always helps mediums to be able to draw on relevant knowledge, skills and experiences from their own pathway.

For instance, can spirit bring in meaningful geographical locations because the medium is well travelled? Or he or she may have served in the army and thus be able to convey accurate information on ranks and regiments? Or if a particular perfume, breed of dog, type of flower or model of car is brought forward by spirit, then the medium may not be able to identify it unless he or she knows about fragrances, canines, botany or automobiles!

Albert Best (1917-1996), a distinguished evidential medium and healer born in Belfast and uncle of international footballer George Best, worked for some years as a postman, delivering letters and parcels in the county of Ayrshire, south-west Scotland. Therefore it was only natural for the spirit world to prove survival by using his expertise and giving him complete names and addresses to put across at public demonstrations of his mediumship.

Absorbing knowledge from the media & arts

It is always going to be easier to talk about something you know rather than about something you don't know. That is why many mediums like to read up and assimilate facts about other people's existences, particularly in documentary programmes, biographies and autobiographies, because such sources open up a lot more for them and improve the depth and quality of information that they are able to pass on. Learning about lives helps with talking about lives!

Essentially, the more broadly based a medium's knowledge is, the better it helps spirits to work with him or her and tell the story that they want to be told.

In a nutshell, mediums will advance the evidence they can provide from spirit by absorbing knowledge like a sponge from the widest possible spectrum of stories, books, films, theatre, arts, music and songs, not to mention the broadcast media.

Using symbols for communicating information

Floral arrangements are especially interesting, because differently coloured floral species are presented as symbols or codes for different family events such as birthdays, christenings, wedding anniversaries or funerals. Equally, the colour of icing, blue or pink, on a celebratory cake can indicate whether a birthday is for a male or female. Two cakes can signify two birthdays in the same month.

Allusion may be made to the mental state of the recipient of the message. An image of a model train set may serve to symbolise that you are currently going around in circles. A depiction of the hedge maze at Hampton Court Palace would indicate that you do not know which way to turn.

As far as the medium Robin Clayton is concerned, bluebells are offered to symbolise love, red roses or white peace lilies are usually to mark the anniversary of a passing, white roses are to celebrate a birthday, and climbing roses may mean an addition to the family. Bright yellow tulips and daffodils suggest that the human recipient needs upliftment or mentoring to improve his or her moral or spiritual condition.

Or a species may be identified simply to describe an actual experience or circumstance involving that flower, for instance the memory of a walk through bluebell woods.

How incoming information is interpreted

Then analogies or parallels are frequently employed for communication, and it becomes a matter of how they are interpreted.

Interpretation can go awry if in their presentations mediums "jump the gun" with hasty and erroneous assumptions. If they work too quickly and rush to get a message out, for example confusing different character traits, feelings and experiences coming in from different spirits and generations within a soul group, then the jumble of facts is bound to baffle or mislead the recipient in the audience too.

The quality of information is far better when mediums are patient and take their time in interpreting it and putting it across carefully and accurately.

If the spirit communicator says that there is a connection with an unspecified seaside resort, then a medium's mind may only be able to visualise and infer Brighton, as the one he or she possibly knows best. Or scaffolding may be depicted to signify construction work currently in progress, rather than a person's historical job in the building trade.

A spirit's gesture in raising a glass may be to celebrate a forthcoming anniversary or special family occasion. Taking off a ring may indicate a marital divide, or a chequered flag may symbolise an ending. Keys may be shown to signify a house move or new life opportunities, a wristwatch to denote the importance of time.

Interestingly, Robin always takes off his watch when doing platform demonstrations, so that he can feel if one is put on his wrist by spirit, to indicate that the spirit wore one during their earthly life.

The opening of a flower's petals can signify the maturing of young people. If say half-a-dozen blooms are visualised to the medium, this may refer to six relatives either on earth or in spirit.

Or, if the touch and smell of a particular type of employment activity is described, is it one which the medium can recognise from his or her own past?

Like a battery draining of energy

Towards the end of a session or sitting, for the medium it can be like "last orders at the bar" or "a classroom of schoolchildren speaking simultaneously", because a coach party of spirits will crowd forward to use the opportunity to communicate

Two sample spirit portraits drawn by the famous British spirit artist and medium Coral Polge, compared to actual photographs of the same individuals juxtaposed on the right.

Born in Hackney, London, Coral Polge lived from 1924 to 2001

messages.

Thereafter spirits know exactly when the mind of the medium is getting tired, and his or her energy is draining like a battery, and will step back to close the communication session. They need to use the medium's own energy to some degree or other in every form of mediumship. For that reason two mediums will often function better if together on a platform and relay more accurate messages, with one resting and replenishing energy while the other is busy working.

When Robin is communicating with the spirit guide Alfred, it is in a deeper, semi-trance state where there is more to concentrate upon from Alfred, and less of Robin's own mind comes into play. As a result, the energy drain from half-an-hour of communication with Alfred is the equivalent of fully 90 minutes with members of my family in spirit, when Robin's own knowledge and life experiences will permeate and reinforce the dialogue with less effort.

The diversity of psychic & spiritual messaging

Psychic messaging is quite distinct from the spirit-to-spirit communication practised by evidential mediums. A psychic or telepathic reading of someone's life story is not spirit-to-spirit but is performed instead by psychics when sitting within and tapping into the subject's electromagnetic energy field or aura. Chapter 12 discusses the workings of the human aura in more detail.

Not every psychic is a medium, but every medium is a psychic. In the latter case, the medium absolutely needs to know the difference between a psychic link and a mediumistic or spirit link, and when incoming evidence is being redirected by a willing spirit from one to the other.

Psychic readings are commonly performed, whereby a medium interprets what you think is your purely random choice of physical objects and symbols. They may be cards (cartomancy), tea leaves (tasseography), numbers (numerology), crystals, flowers, coloured ribbons, and even sand and seeds, explaining the relevance of your choice to your life's journey. However, the personal and private details that may be forthcoming make such readings far more suited to one-to-one sittings than public demonstrations.

Spirit art requires no artistic skills

Spirit art is another type of messaging, a fascinating experiment which can bring excellent visual evidence, linked in with a description of the life, character and health of the person depicted. Or such art may comprise intricate, highly creative colour images called auragraphs which then need to be interpreted.
More complex messages too can be portrayed, with drawings that tell a story.

In essence, spirit controls what is drawn by the medium, who need not possess any artistic skills at all. He or she is inspired by a spirit coming near to create shapes and colours instinctively in a particular way, and the image is formed as the pen, pencil or brush moves across the paper.

Sometimes the drawing or painting is a likeness of an individual who has passed to spirit, so that the medium draws a portrait of the spirit he or she links with and visualises. Spirit guides (discussed later) can also be depicted by this process.

Portrait of Frederic Myers (1843-1901) by William Clarke Wontner

The trance medium Mrs Leonora Piper of Boston, Massachusetts

Taking just one example, the hand of the acclaimed South Wales physical medium Alexander Frederick (Alec) Harris (1897-1974) appeared to be controlled as he drew accurate likenesses of the spirit guides who had previously materialised to his séance group, after forming from his body's ectoplasm. I explain physical mediumship and ectoplasm shortly.

Automatic spirit writing

A technique similar to spirit art for getting messages from the spirit world – on your own and without the need for a medium – is psychography or automatic spirit writing, whether by pen and paper or keyboard.

So you dash off messages before you have chance to think about what you are putting down – without reading them back at the time or considering spelling or grammar. Typically you can ask questions in your mind or on paper and scribble whatever answers pop into your head. Thus prompted by spirit, the style and content will be very different to those of your normal writing.

The process is one of shutting off your conscious or thinking mind so as to allow your unconscious mind to take over what you are composing.

A picture taken by Daily Mirror photographer Leon Isaacs, under infra-red filtered light in a blacked-out room, of the entranced Welsh physical medium, former Swansea miner Jack Webber (1907-40). It was included in a report on this séance published on pages 16 and 17 of the Daily Mirror issue of 28th February 1939.

During the sitting at 11 Childebert Road, Balham, London SW17, spirit is levitating a table weighing 20kg (44lb), scattering individual books from it in different directions.

Jack's first séance in London had been at the home of the President of the Hendon Spiritualist Fellowship on 21st April 1938: he had arrived the same day from his home town of Loughor near Swansea.

Another published photograph of physical medium Jack Webber in trance state, taken by Leon Isaacs under infra-red filtered light in early November 1938, again at 11 Childebert Road. Bound firmly to a chair for his demonstration of direct voice mediumship, Jack Webber is projecting rods of white ectoplasm from his mouth and solar plexus which support two spirit trumpets simultaneously in mid-air. Immediately after the picture was taken, spirit sent the trumpets whirling around the darkened séance room at some speed.

An intermediary spirit able to provide the specialised automatic writing skillset is often (but not always) required between the spirit communicator and the physical person who puts pen to paper. Obvious differences in handwriting style, grammar and spelling from message to message show that intermediaries swap around. They would seem to be "volunteers in training" from the spirit world eager to acquire personal knowledge and experience of the art.

Automatic writing in history

Harking back in history, Frederic William Henry Myers, a Professor of Classics at Cambridge University and founder member of the Society for Psychical Research (SPR) in 1882, sent some 12,000 pages of automatic writing over a 30-year period from the spirit world to different direct writing mediums in England, USA and India as proof of his own life after death.

Another founder member of the SPR was Dr Richard Hodgson (1855-1905), originally of the University of Melbourne and whose automatic writing after his passing came through the American trance medium Mrs Leonora Evelina Piper, née Simonds, of Boston (1857-1950).

Mrs Piper's mental and trance mediumship was scientifically tested and proved remarkably consistent. In fact the SPR as a psychic investigations group conducted many sittings with her over two decades. The details and commentary on these experiments were published regularly in the Society's Proceedings, now preserved in the Cambridge University Library as described in Chapter 1.

In Chapter 1 I also referred to the historical strength of the spiritist movement in Brazil. Its chief exponent there became Chico Xavier (1910-2002), a medium, author and philanthropist famous for his prodigious output of poetry, novels, stories, essays and philosophical works which he had received from spirit as inspirational writing. He never accepted payment for anything he wrote, instead donating all of his royalties to charitable causes.

Another example is that of William Thomas Stead, an English newspaper editor, journalist and pacifist, who was born in Northumberland in 1849 and went down with the Titanic in April 1912 after helping women and children into the lifeboats.

In his day Stead had used his automatic writing skills to convey messages from a late American journalist friend in Illinois, Julia Ames. After his drowning, his own automatic writing from spirit was then channelled from 1917 into the 1930s through different mediums, initially through Pardoe Woodman, a young career acquaintance of his daughter Estelle.

Independent direct voice medium Leslie Flint, 1911–1994

***Image by courtesy of the Leslie Flint Educational Trust,* www.leslieflint.com**

Some other forms of mediumship

Because different mediums work at different mental depths and vibrational levels, they will communicate different information. The next, more advanced stage of mediumship is trance communication, an altered state of consciousness where a spirit or spirit guide can completely take over a medium's faculties and speak through him or her with their own voice.

Then some more uncommon and advanced types of mediumship that you will not exactly find in your Yellow Pages are physical mediumship in general and a form of this known as direct voice mediumship. These types often operate away from public gaze in small dedicated groups or home circles over long periods of time.

Physical mediumship uses different energies to other types of mediumship and requires specialist conditions. Participants are seated in an open circle to concentrate spirit energy, working either in the dark or sitting in red light. This supports the production of ectoplasm and the movement of objects around the room.

Physical mediumship

Physical mediumship allows a spirit person to re-form their entire physical body (or, if they employ less energy, only part of their body, such as a hand) from an extrusion of ectoplasm from the medium, with their overall appearance and dress just as on earth, and be seen by everyone present.

A specific form of such materialisation, whereby the spirit communicator uses ectoplasm to mould his or her face and features over the face of the medium like a mask, is known as transfiguration. Usually in transfiguration the faces just show themselves and do not speak. But sometimes a highly developed transfiguration medium goes into deep trance, and spirits are able to create a voicebox, through which to speak, out of ectoplasm from the medium.

In general, the development of physical mediumship skills can stretch over a long and tedious initiation period, with nothing happening in a home circle for months or even years, so that the process requires great dedication and perseverance on everyone's part.

Independent direct voice mediumship

Independent direct voice meanwhile is one of the rarest and most interesting forms of deep physical mediumship, where the voice of a spirit speaks to all those present out of mid-air, independently of the medium. This is often done using a freely floating conical horn, a sound-amplifying séance trumpet, within which spirit energies are concentrated as ectoplasm emanating from the medium. The séance trumpet is simply used as an amplifier, as an ear trumpet was used historically by the hearing impaired.

A Londoner Leslie Flint became one of the most celebrated independent direct voice mediums of the 20th century. Instead of a horn device, he employed an artificial voicebox or larynx which spirit formed from his personal ectoplasm for their communicators to directly speak through.

This unique voicebox, shaped from the ectoplasm and energy physically exuded by Flint's own body, hovered at a distance from him in the darkened séance room. Other sitters present provided the naturally occurring energy from their physical bodies to fuel and support the production of his ectoplasm, as well as conversing with the spirits who came through.

Among Leslie Flint's amazing séance communications, in over a hundred recordings of varying lengths now preserved by the Leslie Flint Educational Trust, Sir Winston Churchill chose to speak via this process in October 1987, Sir Arthur Conan Doyle in January 1966, Dame Ellen Terry and George Bernard Shaw in 1965, and Mahatma Gandhi in July 1961 (www.leslieflint.com/recordings-archive).

A library of Leslie Flint's extraordinary recordings of the voices of people in the afterlife is available at:

http://adcguides.com/librarynames.htm

The virtuoso Polish pianist and composer Frédéric Chopin became a regular, enthusiastic communicator at Flint's séances. He was first recorded speaking at an experimental sitting in 1953, leading to numerous further communications over decades. On 17th October 1955 Chopin talked to Flint's regular musical sitter Rose Creet about his own passing on that day in 1849 and how he was greeted in the afterlife by beautiful music as well as by instrumentalists whom he had known:

https://archive.org/details/ChopinOct17th1955LFT

The first known case in which direct spirit voices were captured by recording equipment dates back half-a-century earlier, to 1901. Obviously this was all dependent upon the technology for recording available in a particular, pre-digital era.

Blending of energies for trance communication

More usually, since spirits do not possess vocal chords, in order to speak audibly they need to use those of a medium and speak through him or her, a process of channelling that has existed since antiquity. Thus in trance communication the actual voice of a companion, compatible spirit guide speaks through the lips of the medium. The human element, reflecting the medium's own ego, personality and life experiences, is taken right out of the equation, and his or her mind plays no role.

Particularly noted for their spirituality in their physical lives, Native Americans are frequently the guise adopted by spirit guides who like to convey important philosophical wisdom on the ways of the world through trance mediums. But in all cases the spirit guides would have lived that particular life.

Well-known examples in Britain have included Silver Birch (via Maurice Barbanell), Black Cloud (Jack Webber), Red Cloud (Estelle Roberts), White Eagle (Grace Cooke) and White Feather (Robert Goodwin). Notably the face of her guide Red Cloud did sometimes materialise in ectoplasm to the physical medium Estelle Roberts and her circle of sitters, during séances held in London over decades from the 1920s on.

Statements of Silver Birch from spirit

Here we quote one of Silver Birch's erudite statements, through Maurice Barbanell, against the pervasive materialism of human kind: "The great ones of your world are not the great ones of my world. We see greatness as greatness of soul, greatness of spirit, greatness in desire to serve. These things will endure long after the glitter of the material world has disappeared."

Silver Birch on religions: "There is no religion higher than service. To heal the sick, to comfort the mourner, to guide the perplexed, to give strength to the weary and direction to those who have lost their way, those are the most important tasks of all. Never forget that the supreme purpose of life is the unfoldment of the spirit."

And two more of his illuminating comments – on love, death and the return home to spirit:

"Know that the one you love and who loves you has left you physically but not spiritually. Death has no power to separate those whom love has joined together and made them one in spirit."

"There is weeping when people die in your world, but there is rejoicing in ours.

Death usually means that the life has served its purpose . . . and the individual is ready to enjoy all the tremendous richness and beauty that the spirit life has to offer."

The English trance medium and magazine editor Maurice Barbanell (1902–1981) and Silver Birch, his Native American spirit guide throughout his life. The Spiritualists' National Union (SNU) organisation has renamed its regional conference centre at Stafford after Barbanell.

No secrets exist between spirits

Operating at a far deeper and more physically and mentally demanding level for mediums, trance mediumship enables spirit to convey more information than is possible through regular evidential, spirit-to-spirit mediumship. There are no secrets between spirits in the spirit world – information flows freely.

Accordingly, by this trance technique, you can dig a lot deeper, in order to find out about the past lives and spirit guides of mortals just as easily as those of spirit entities. Previous lives are, however, not just on public show, as it were, to another spirit: they do need to be interrogated for a valid purpose.

Moreover, what insight can be gained from a trance sitting is dependent on the particular understanding and opinion of the spirit who chooses to use a given medium as a mouthpiece or, put more crudely, "an empty vessel". The energy of the spirit and that of the medium are variables in the equation – they need to blend exactly and form a symbiotic relationship or union. They will generally share a common view of the world and common convictions.

Energy and vibration are bound to vary from one spirit to another, and depending on what stage they have reached so far in their spiritual progression or journey. But when such success is achieved in blending, the trance medium and spirit become entirely comfortable with each other and can generally maintain a relationship of many years.

Coming out of trance sessions, even more so than with other mediumistic sittings, the medium will recall very little of what he or she has actually said. During a session, the medium will have perceived the voice of the spirit as muffled and appearing to emanate remotely, as it were, from an adjoining room, rather than from his or her own mouth.

Access to mediums

In general, one of the practical problems is that access to established mediums is very limited, and members of the general public (unless brought along by a spiritualist relative, friend or neighbour) are apprehensive about attending platform demonstrations of mediumship laid on in spiritualist churches. Spiritualists are widely regarded as a "closed community", adherents of some sort of fringe faith, much like others you encounter in premises along main street.

As in my own case, the motivation to first visit a medium is generally to open up a line of – or a portal or window for – communication with a recently deceased loved one.

It is recorded that, the year after King George VI passed from a sudden coronary thrombosis at Sandringham on 6th February 1952, aged just 56, the British royal family privately consulted a leading female trance medium of that era, Cardiff-born Lilian Bailey, to find out if the late monarch had any instructions or advice for them. But we shall never know what was said at that séance in Kensington, London, in 1953.

Then there are of course fraudulent mediums and fortune-tellers about, whose aim has always been to make money from the gullible or grieving. Most of us will have come across those dubious end-of-pier booths with a list out front of supposedly satisfied celebrity clients!

Phoney mediums are now covered in the UK by consumer protection legislation, namely the "Consumer Protection from Unfair Trading" Regulations 2008, which replaced the Fraudulent Mediums Act of 1951. Respected spiritualist organisations and news media regard the elimination of bogus operators as being of paramount importance.

Chapter 9

SENSING ENERGIES & SPIRITS

Distinguishing between different energies

For perhaps the first six months of regular communication, to assist recognition a spirit communicator will project into the medium's mind an identifiable image of itself in human form, with a certain age, appearance and dress from a particular past life. Thereafter that image is unnecessary and not provided, so that the spirit's energy alone from its last human life becomes a sufficient identifier. The blending of energies between medium and spirit over time builds familiarity, trust and relaxed communication.

In their role of "serving spirit", spiritualist mediums can distinguish between different spirits by their different energies which they feel. The essence or quality of a given spirit's energy will remain recognisable to any medium as the same spirit, even as it evolves and progresses to higher vibrations. We do not notice subtle changes over time in people whom we see regularly, and so it is with the slow and gradual evolution of spirits who come through recurrently to mediums.

Despite the spirit communicator having neither gender nor age, to feel and describe customary physical characteristics of the sexes can be helpful, if the spirit perceives that that is how a given medium works. Feminine, emotional, loving and gentle energy is differentiated from stronger, brasher and more forceful masculine energy.

A blood relative will come through on a stronger energy – bringing heightened emotion – than a friend relationship, and a close relative will be distinguishable from a more distant one. The medium feels greater emotion and a more loving parental feeling the closer the blood relationship is.

Personality & health attributes from the physical life

Spirit energies come across to mediums as serious or light-hearted, nervous or relaxed, extrovert or introvert, affectionate or standoffish, etc, and by the mind picture they get of the physical appearance with which the soul or spirit wishes to come forward. The latter would include their racial type, skin colour, sex, age, height, build, hairstyle, facial hair and clothing.

Habits, likes and dislikes, health condition, mannerisms and personality traits – carrying on from the souls' lives on the earth plane – can all be identified as memories from spirit. When in human form, did they show love and emotions outwardly or were they emotionally closed? Were they modern or old-fashioned in outlook and dress? Were they sociable or solitary, dependent or independent, laconic or garrulous, assertive or vacillating, patient or impatient, considerate or unthinking? Did they have rough or smooth hands? What rings or watches did they wear?

The other possibility is for the personae from a soul's past lives to siphon through. Little bits of information can come through in this way which may not be immediately intelligible. I go on to discuss reincarnation and previous lives at a later stage.

Spirits team up & combine energies

Energy is always the determining factor, whether generated by the spirit entities or by the humans present in the room at the time. An unfamiliar spirit being can be successfully introduced, ushered in, by piggybacking on the energy of another, better known one, hanging onto their coat-tails and utilising their energy.

Moreover combined energy, the brighter light, from the collective consciousness of a number of spirits, or even of a whole soul group, through teamwork, organisation and planning, will attract the attention of the medium more strongly during a sitting or mass platform demonstration.

The process of teaming up is a bit like a globule of mercury, oil or liquid wax moving to merge with another and another and another to form a pool. In this way, spirits will have greater success in commanding attention and successfully "forcing their way to the front of the queue" – if their message is considered vital for the recipient at that time.

Spirit sets the priority for messages

So who in the audience needs a message most – typically the most recently bereaved or most troubled? Accordingly, the precedence or prioritisation of messages from the platform is actually determined by spirit and not, as you may think, by the medium.

Memory evidence may be forthcoming jointly from several loved ones, not just one, so that mediums need to separate and decipher what's what from the mass of energy. In the case of a sizeable combined soul group comprising numerous families and friends, whilst a few spirits will present their images to the medium by way of identification, most of those present will not, instead remaining in the background where they can strengthen the effect of the energy.

In order to put forward a single spokesperson or prime communicator, spirits will however introduce into the medium's mind an identifiable image, at some time of life, of one of their number. The prime communicator can pass on messages from anyone in the soul group and speak on behalf of everyone.

In the same way, exercises to demonstrate the presence of spirit, and the movement of objects – "apports", as I discuss later on – will usually call for such collective spirit energy to be applied.

Bringing spirits close

All spirit entities have freewill to decide whether or not they wish to step forward and speak. They come through not with what we ***want*** but with what we ***need*** at that time, and the medium cannot oblige any particular spirit to draw close.

What we have in our hearts and minds means more than anything, and a strong love relationship with someone still on the earth plane will also encourage a spirit to come through to try to communicate with that person.

Thinking about an ancestor, or looking at a family photo of him or her or sharing favourite music with them, will bring that individual close. Photos, music, cinema and stage performances typically stir memories of experiences shared, and awakening one memory tends to open up our mind to more and more of them.

Chapter 10

HOW WE CAN INTERACT WITH SPIRIT

Psychic versions of the human senses

Many people are familiar with the expressions clairvoyance (clear seeing), clairaudience (clear hearing) and clairsentience (clear feeling), but there are also two other "clairs" that don't get as much attention – clairgustance (clear tasting) and clairsalience (clear smelling).

All of these terms may be traced back to a French aristocrat, the Marquis de Puységur, who pioneered research into the subconscious mind and how the human brain works. He was one of the founders, alongside his mentor, the German physician Franz Mesmer, of the therapeutic science of mesmerism, later renamed as hypnotism.

The Marquis de Puységur, 1751–1825

So our physical senses (seeing, hearing, feeling, tasting, smelling) have an equivalent psychic version, and all of them can be developed.

Accordingly, when performing readings, mediums can employ one or more of those

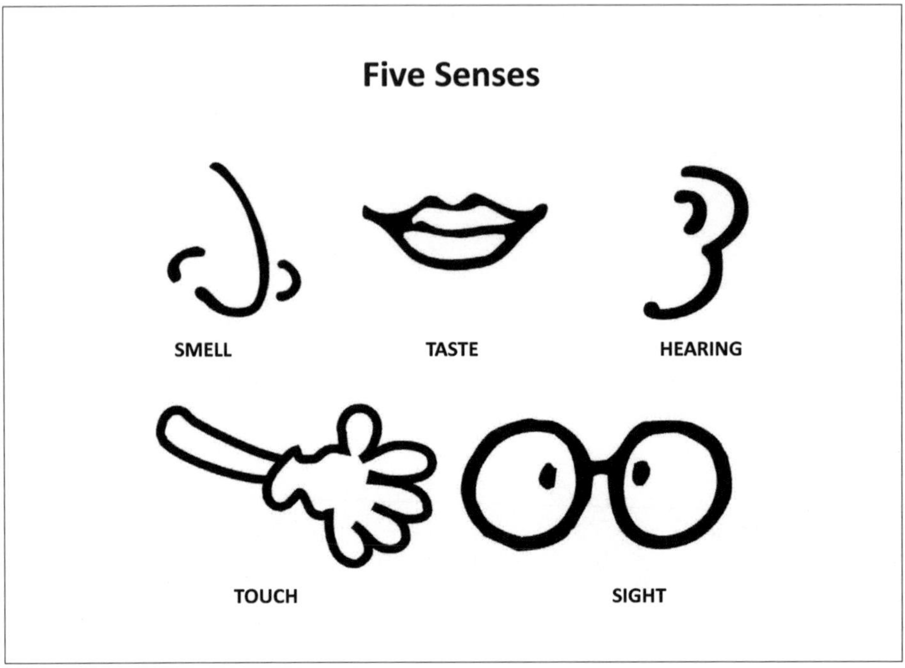

five traditional human senses – sight, hearing, touch, taste, smell. Terminology-wise, clairsentient mediums will feel what the spirit feels, clairaudient ones hear voices, clairgustant ones experience tastes, clairsalient ones smell scents, and clairvoyant mediums see visualisations of spirit in front of them.

The latter does not mean "clairvoyance" in terms of predicting the future, an aptitude outside of evidential mediums' range, unlike the visionaries and seers of history, such as Nostradamus referred to in Chapter 3.

Interpreting the vibrational energy of an object

Further exploring the sense of touch and thus using a blindfold to take sight out of the equation, some people with spiritual leanings are proficient at psychometry. That is the ability to discover facts psychically about a person or his or her historical experiences by handling an inanimate object once intimately connected with that individual, such as a diary, watch or piece of jewellery or clothing.

Such people feel and interpret the residual vibrational energy radiating from the object, as if its history, its life story, is imprinted on it for them to read.

The energy within personal jewellery

Talking further about objects, an interesting aspect of our interaction with spirit is the energy associated with wearing or holding a personal item of jewellery in fond memory of a departed loved one, such as his or her ring, bracelet, bangle, necklace or pendant.

These can have three properties. They can bring the loved one close to you. They can strengthen the energy and happiness level of that spirit. And the energy can help to protect your own health.

The World Hearing Voices Congress

Interestingly, when, as a clairaudient medium, you hear voices in your head and yet never see lip movements, uncertainties will naturally arise in your mind when you have to convey names to an audience or sitter which sound similar. So, clairaudiently, did you hear Taylor or Tyler, Jesse or Jose, Britney or Brittany, Casey or Cassie, Janet or Janice, Mary or Marie?

More broadly, the annual World Hearing Voices Congress delves deeply into that whole subject of particular international fascination, attempting to look beyond a spiritualist clairaudient explanation for it.

Adults can tragically be abused or encouraged to self-harm by voices they hear, reminiscent of a playground bully who exploits the weak spots and insecurities of fellow pupils. To sufferers from this mental affliction, the threatening voices seem very real and ever-present.

So the psychiatric jury is still out on how and why this happens, hence the Congress. The event switches between different cities, with the 11th Congress having been staged at Montreal, Canada, in November 2019 and the 12th at Cork, Irish Republic, in September 2021.

Synchronicity of vibration, time & place

Our experience of, for example, voices and complete materialisations will demand synchronicity of the right vibration, time and place, principally where the spirit is choosing a denser energy and slower vibration more in tune with ours. A spirit person needs to concentrate a large amount of energy to fully materialise, rather than appear as a misty outline or a brief glimpse.

Spirits will tend to materialise or project themselves in a form you would immediately recognise and be comfortable with, whereas another person next to you whose mind is not correctly attuned would not see the image. Accordingly spirits can imprint their familiar physical form on our consciousness, using the faculties of our minds and what we may remember from the past. And there is no way that they would wish to frighten or startle us either!

Spirits and spirit guides get to know which mediums they can best work with. In cases where a medium, being empathetic, can resonate or gel well with a given spirit, then communication can be far easier and more productive and successful. Compatible energies are attracted to each other like magnets.

Thus, for example, loud spirits will prefer to communicate through mediums possessing a similarly loud and extrovert personality. It is ideal if the medium can have an emotional rapport or common interests and shared sense-of-humour with the spirit who chooses to come through.

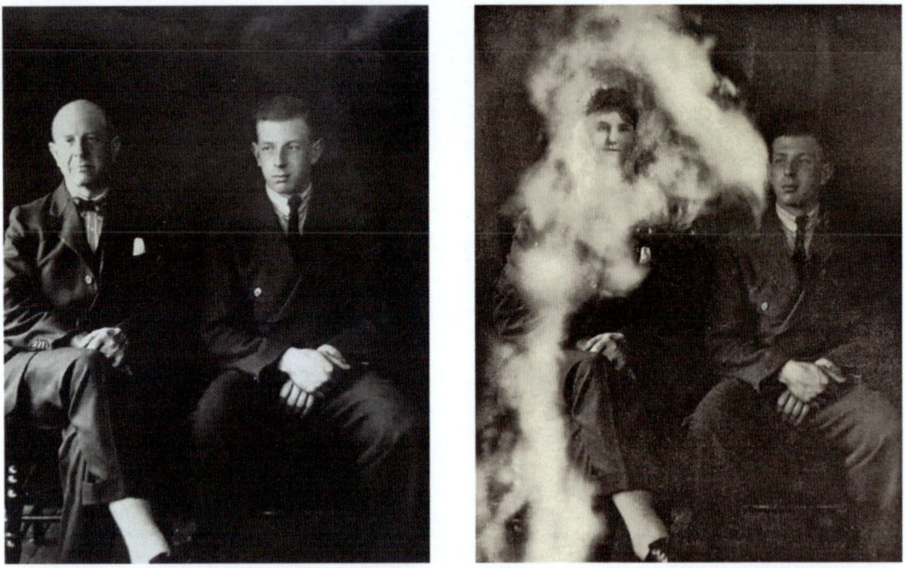

The face of an unidentified spirit lady physically materialised within a cloud in this photograph of a father Ralph (left) and son Charles (right) of the Cooke family, taken at a professional studio in the town of Wigan, Lancashire, UK, in early 1928. All parties involved – the subjects, the photographer and the photographic processor in the region of their family home in the village of Annfield Plain, County Durham – authenticated the picture. Prior to this era, for over a century generations of the Cookes had lived above their shop in the main street there, a clothing emporium Ralph sold in 1903. The first ever authenticated spirit photograph was captured by a jewellery engraver William H Mumler of Boston, USA, in 1861, whilst the first fully verifiable one in Britain was by a photographer called Hudson in March 1872.

Chapter 11

OTHER ASPECTS OF MEDIUMS' WORK

Spirit attachments released by mediums

In the case of a spirit attachment, an experienced medium may actually witness a discarnate dark entity feeding off a living person's physical energy field or aura, much like a parasite on their shoulder. The medium can then carry out the straightforward task of releasing that entity – persuading it to relocate to the spirit world where it belongs – and restore light around the person.

Long-established spirit attachments may in some cases be benign and not cause any problems to a human host. Attachment occurs in the first place allegedly when a person passes away and yet becomes earthbound owing to strong emotional ties, unfinished business, or a total unawareness of their own passing. Spirits may need to get things off their chest to enable them to progress.

According to this premise, intelligent, scared and troubled earthbound spirits, or indeed so-called elementals of low intelligence – low-level earthbound entities, can be attracted at random to a vulnerable human host who fills their vicarious needs, or even jump from one person to another.

Symptoms of attachment may include extreme mood fluctuations, chronic fatigue, alcohol or drug abuse, and physical damage to pre-existing weak spots in the human body. An argument commonly heard is that, if you are addicted for example to alcohol, then you will attract the earthbound spirit of someone who was an alcoholic.

The severity of the symptoms depends upon how fully the entity invades the consciousness and body of the host, possibly calling for the services of a practised medium. Few indicators of any sort may show up in the instance of more neutral or even benevolent attachments.

Work in quietening houses

Mediums will also be invited by residents into houses to resolve issues there of restless spirits perhaps appearing by children's beds or moving small objects about telekinetically.

Such paranormal problems are often caused by the frustration of past family members, such as grandparents, at not being able to let their nearest and dearest know in any other way that they are OK, and are around them and still loving and supporting them emotionally. Or spirits may be greatly troubled by a change that has happened to their family on earth and not understand the reason for it.

Relatives on earth may simply not be open to a spirit's attempted mental communications, but the medium can find out what those communications consist of and successfully pass them on, to placate the spirit and restore peace, putting the household "back on the straight and narrow".

Ghosts are recurring images stuck in time

That is quite different to the phenomena which we describe variously as ghosts, apparitions, spectres, wraiths, phantoms or revenants. They are recurring images caught or stuck in human time and seemingly in the very fabric of old buildings and sites.

Unlike a spirit, a ghost, although composed of indestructible energy, is not a living energy and has no intellect. A spirit can interact and communicate with a medium, answer questions and lead us to do things, whereas ghosts cannot. They are completely different to rare, actual materialisations of spirit.

Accordingly a medium cannot talk to a ghost and persuade it to cease its particular activity, which may be repeated ad infinitum at the same location. The spirit once associated with a ghostly image will be long gone to the spirit world and be safe and sound there, or may indeed have been reincarnated on earth as someone completely different.

An old site's resident ghosts, by tradition traumatised or tormented figures, are composed of pure energy and cannot communicate with us, and yet anyone receptive enough can see them and even photograph them. Their energy can take many forms, but requires a solid base such as a building, floor or hard ground to react against and hence not get dissipated or attenuated.

Residual hauntings can repeat on a loop

Typically for so-called residual hauntings, ghosts are engaged in a particular repetitive activity. Oblivious to any observers, they go about their business in a set way, as if scripted in a movie.

And so you get "grey ladies" in antiquated clothing from centuries ago appearing at windows or in churchyards, phantom horsemen and monks, or Roman soldiers marching through rooms at knee height because the floor was originally that much lower.

Indeed, ghostly apparitions have often been witnessed over the years haunting famous British battlefield sites, from Bosworth Field, Culloden and Edgehill to Flodden, Naseby and Sedgemoor, not to mention the well documented American Civil War ghosts of Gettysburg, Pennsylvania and Cold Harbor, Virginia.

All such manifestations are "imprinted in the ether" as it were and may be endlessly repeated like a videotape playing on a loop, always viewed the same.

Not everyone present will see the ghost, but those receptive enough will see an identical image. Ghosts can appear to us at a particular location to mark the anniversary of an event there that, although hugely significant to those individuals, is now most likely lost in history.

Raising & combining natural energy

When giving messages for instance to members of a live audience from a platform, the medium's communication with spirit is also greatly helped by a positive ambience such as a happy and bubbly, even euphoric, atmosphere and upbeat music to lift people's mood and raise the collective energies in the room.

A concentration or uplift of natural energy within a space, such as from human, animal or plant life, is attractive to spirit beings and important to them.

Combined energy will always achieve more. Healing teams of spirit energies, now including my wife Pam, a fully fledged reiki practitioner in her physical life, support spiritual healers on earth who work to improve an individual's health. Furthermore, as we know, combined human energy pulls spirits closer to stimulate our communication with them.

Similarly but on a grander scale, people are immersed and carried along by the energy generated, and possibly an adrenalin rush, in attending a concert, rave, stadium sport, political rally or large-scale religious event. Meanwhile endorphins produced in those circumstances by our central nervous system and pituitary gland can give us a general feeling of happiness, amusement or even euphoria.

Music as an effective catalyst

Simply listening to the right sort of music, or singing along in a relaxed manner, will raise the energy and morale of a person without making demands on their brain to be active or busy.

Music can be especially effective as a catalyst, resonating with us and moving us emotionally. If you allow yourself to get immersed in a particular song or track which takes you out of yourself, then arguably you "become the energy" of that song. It may encourage you to tap your feet or move to the beat as you engage your feelings.

Certain bars of music, tracks and instruments can heighten our emotions and open up our awareness to the presence of spirits around us, bringing tears to our eyes if we are empathetic by nature.

Different pieces are characterised by different vibrations, and certain vibrations make you more aware of loved ones being around. That is not the same experience as songs or tunes holding particular memories, shared by you and them irrespective of vibrations.

The strength of ambient spiritual energy

And so, whilst some folk radiate uplifting, positive energy with love, humour and laughter, bringing sunshine to your life, others around you will exhibit negative energy and melancholy, sapping your vitality, draining you and making you physically tired.

We have all encountered grumpy and morose characters whose world view is intrinsically pessimistic and cynical. Indeed the predominant energy in a room can easily change from positive to negative, for instance if a quarrel breaks out between people.

Furthermore, as soon as you move away from social contact and interaction and are on your own once more, then your own personal energy field drops by natural process.

By contrast, ambient spiritual energy does not just dissipate in the ether. In the same way that natural, straight, ley lines with a stronger electromagnetic footprint run across our landscape, so spiritual energy can be stronger in some environments than others. It can accumulate steadily over time in the atmosphere of a particular meeting room, auditorium, hall, place of worship or other building, because of the energy footprint that we all leave behind.

The chief determinant for creating mass spiritual energy is the participants' unified thought built around a single purpose – a battle, mass religious experience (such as at Fátima, Portugal, in October 1917), football game, street rally, music event, movie, play, and so forth. It is not the same as inside say London's busiest railway station, Waterloo, despite its 100 million recorded entries and exits a year. That is because those millions are carrying many and varied personal thoughts and preoccupations, with hardly any common denominator except the act of travelling.

Thus the build-up of spiritual energy occurs where large numbers of people regularly meet for a single, defined objective, and can remain in place to aid for example future interaction with spirit.

The effect of peace lilies on atmosphere

Another influence I have discovered from spirits' feedback which genuinely does create a welcoming and comforting atmosphere for them, although it is difficult to explain why, is the presence of air-purifying tropical houseplants called peace lilies (botanically: spathiphyllum).

All that we really know is that the peace lily is so effective at cleaning the air that NASA recommended it for use on the International Space Station (ISS). Of all the houseplants which NASA tested, the peace lily species was the most effective one at removing the toxic substances benzene, formaldehyde, xylene, toluene and trichloroethylene from the air.

The seven principles

There are seven principles in spiritualism viewed as a religion. These go back 150 years to Victorian England and Emma Hardinge Britten, the remarkable pioneer described in Chapter 1. However, despite their obvious historical value, they are limited in scope and correspond only partly with the reality of the spirit world as we now know it to be. Our understanding has frankly moved on. For the record, the principles are as follows:

1. The fatherhood of God.
2. The brotherhood of Man.
3. The communion of spirits and ministry of angels.
4. The continuous existence of the human soul.
5. Personal responsibility.
6. Compensation and retribution hereafter for all good and evil deeds done on earth.
7. Eternal progress open to every human soul.

An organisation called the Spiritualists' National Union (SNU), founded in the UK on 18th October 1901, adopted these seven principles and promotes them in its broad network of churches, where it holds religious services and other spiritualist events open to the public.

Glasgow-born James Arthur Findlay, MBE, JP was a writer, accountant, stockbroker and Essex magistrate, as well as being a significant figure in the history of spiritualism from the 1920s to the 1940s. In his will he generously left his palatial family home and estate, Stansted Hall in Essex, to the Spiritualists' National Union to become its de facto headquarters, administered by the Union as a residential college for the advancement of spiritualism and psychic science.

Another organisation, the Spiritualist Association of Great Britain (SAGB), with its origins in the Marylebone Spiritualist Association founded in 1872 and based nowadays in Battersea, London, upholds its own set of seven religious principles.

Even so, its emphasis is similarly on the continuity of existence and eternal progress in the afterlife and our responsibility for the way we conduct our earthly lives. Sir Arthur Conan Doyle and Air Chief Marshal Lord Dowding, both referred to in Chapter 1, were prominent supporters of the SAGB.

James Arthur Findlay, 1883-1964 **www.arthurfindlaycollege.org**

The duty to exercise personal responsibility

Of the seven principles listed above, three at least are relevant to our discussion in this book. Thus we have "the continuous existence of the human soul" (4) and "the eternal progress open to every human soul" (7). But also the exercise of "personal responsibility" (5), because it is incumbent upon mediums and spiritualists not to cause distress to their fellow humans by the knowledge they acquire from spirit.

The responsibility for any message lies partly with the spirit communicator – concerned not to upset a recipient and wishing to communicate a dramatic message only when people are around to support that person emotionally. But also the medium may have to censor or sanitise a message, for example not betraying too much personal information from the platform nor unduly frightening people with health prognoses.

Clearly mediums can be unthinking and irresponsible enough to "blow people's minds" with the information they impart. I heard of a fake, money-making operator in Yardley, Birmingham, UK, who of course made an elderly lady terribly upset by telling her that she was going to die soon. Yes, with the power and authority they have in conveying messages from spirit to the physical world, legitimate mediums must at all times exercise personal responsibility.

Chapter 12

AURAS & CHAKRAS

Interpreting the human aura

The communication link used by evidential mediums should be genuinely spirit-to-spirit and not merely psychic or telepathic, such as an aura reading traditionally used by psychics when sitting within a subject's energy field. An aura or electromagnetic energy field is an emanation enclosing every living thing in bands of colour and totally specific to the individual being.

Through a personal interpretation of your aura, its colours, brightness and size range, bona fide psychics can deduce many things – your character strengths and weaknesses, talents, mental harmony, health, emotions, relationships, working life and the energy you exude (motivating, guiding or inspiring those around you, for example).

Psychics can possess the ability to actually see the size, colours and type of vibration of an aura, and the phenomenon can be captured by Kirlian aura photography as an electromagnetic emanation. Such photography is usually best done at intervals of several months, in order to observe the changes which arise in an individual's aura as his or her life evolves.

Kirlian aura photography

Kirlian photography is named after the Soviet inventor and researcher Semyon Kirlian, who in 1939 discovered that, if an object is put onto a photographic plate to which a high-voltage electrical current is then applied, the image produced on the plate shows that object surrounded by a bright luminous aura. The process was patented by the Soviet Union under Stalin in 1949 and yet did not achieve its proper recognition in the USA and Western world for another 20 years, after the fundamentals of the technology had been stumbled upon and translated from Russian into English.

Some people can see certain colours in auras more than others. The higher the vibration, the brighter are all the colours.

The human aura may have positive or negative vibrations, depending upon the conduct, mental state, thought pattern and character of the person. If the person is positive, the aura will be positive, but if he or she is negative, vibrations of his or her aura will also be negative.

A striking Kirlian photograph of the electromagnetic aura around a living trifoliate plant leaf
www.fengshuidana.com

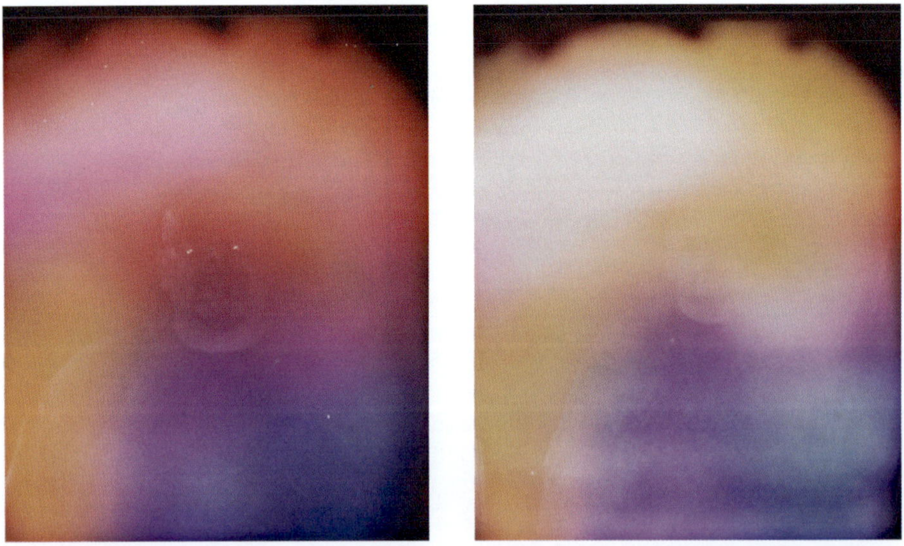

Robin Clayton's aura photographed in October 2003 (left) and May 2004 (right) at Stansted Hall, Essex, by Thelma Francis, a medium and one of the tutors of the Arthur Findlay College there

Chakra energy centres

In New Age alternative medicine, the human aura, the energy field of the body, is regarded as a hidden anatomy which directly affects health. It comprises seven non-physical energy centres called chakras, which tie in to some extent with the body's endocrine system – the various glands that secrete hormones into our cardiovascular system. Human beings have the ability to expand their auric or energy field outwards to fill the space around them.

The aura reflects the ups and downs experienced over the individual's entire lifetime on earth and may be read or interpreted in different ways for different reasons, with scope for human error, depending on how many years of experience the interpreter possesses.

Each different layer of the auric field, composed as mentioned above of non-physical energy, has its own particular function and is associated with a chakra. Denser and slower energy is closest to the body and easier to detect, whilst lighter and faster energy is progressively further away.

Each chakra is associated with a primary gender, or masculine or feminine energy, although a chakra is never completely male or female. Unlike male and female

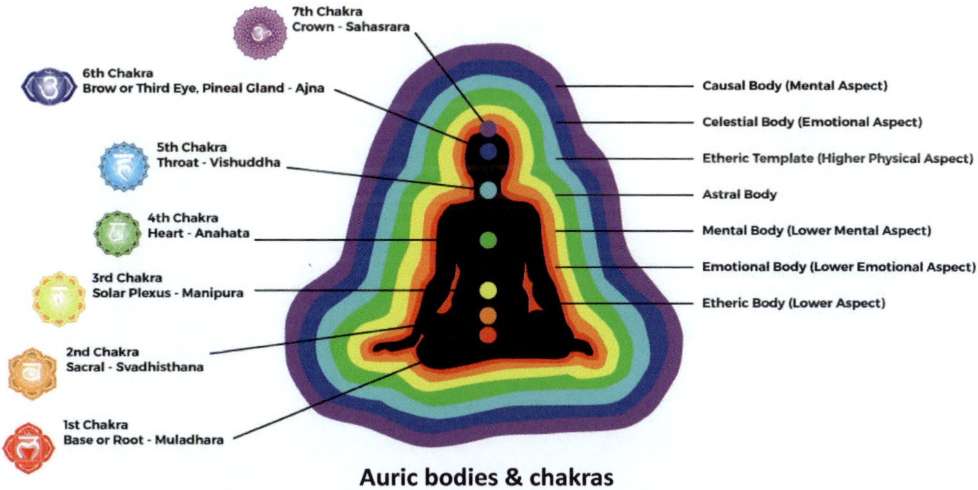

Auric bodies & chakras

Image source: www.kea0.com/human-aura-and-benefit-of-seeing-aura/

as a sexual gender, these energies embody a quality or essence instead. The predominantly female essence (yin or in Hinduism Shakti) represents dark, passive and receptive energy, whereas the male equivalent (yang, in Hinduism Shiva) epitomises light, active and penetrative energy.

The notion is that, when chakras "become blocked" or vibrations go out of synchronisation, then health problems will arise for the individual.

The colours of the chakras are related to the seven basic energy centres in the body. From the head downwards, the chakras are: violet, indigo, blue, green, yellow, orange and red.

The sound of colours

And, interestingly, each chakra is associated with a physical sound or note in the musical scale. Since every colour has a different vibration (see Chapter 3), different paintings, images or even faces have a different note or sound.

Neil Harbisson from the London Borough of Camden was born with a medical condition that means he can only see in black-and-white. So he decided to wear a cybernetic device (an audio input chip implanted inside the back of his head plus a head-mounted camera) which converts colours into sound waves. Colour

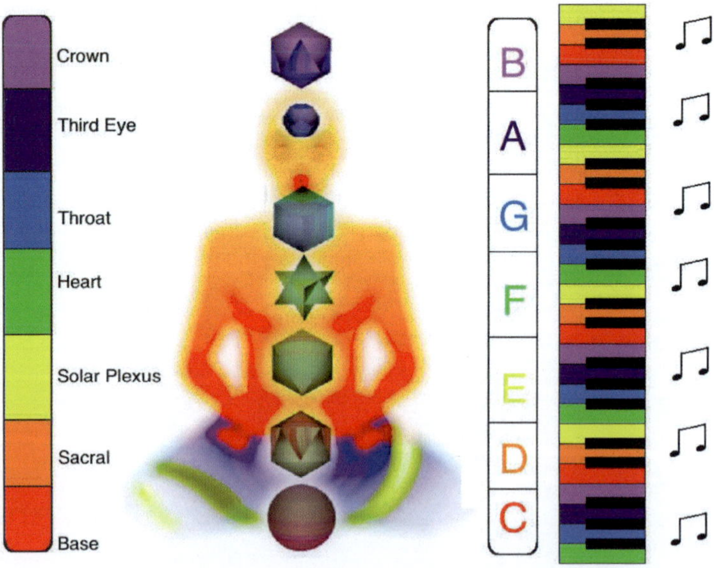

The seven chakras with accompanying musical notes

Image source: www.kea0.com

frequencies are transposed to sound frequencies.

A wi-fi connector inside the chip allows him to hear, for example, images sent from a mobile phone – without even looking at them. The implant, inserted by surgeons in a world first operation in Barcelona, means that Harbisson can now hear a symphony of colours in a microtonal sonochromatic scale, instead of seeing the world only in greyscale.

Using your mind's eye

Of particular significance is the so-called "third eye chakra" of colour indigo. Located between the eyebrows and on your forehead (your "mind's eye" in Hinduism, Buddhism or Jainism, also known as "Ajna" in Sanskrit) and accordingly between the two hemispheres of your brain, the "third eye" is the centre of intuition and spiritual insight, providing perception beyond normal vision.

In fact, to stare without blinking at a bright, shining object, to cover your eyes with your palms, and then to practise at maintaining the afterimage in your mind's eye without it fading, are steps in a common exercise used to develop the image-making faculty of budding psychics.

The Ajna chakra between the eyebrows is also associated with the pineal gland in that part of the brain (see Chapter 2 above), and Hindus noticeably apply a vermilion red dot or bindi to the spot, sacred to their religion.

So, particularly when close up to you, a psychic has the ability to use his or her "third eye" to read and tell you what is encoded in your energy field or chakras. But, whilst impressive enough, such psychic reading, often dressed up as telepathy, is not spiritual mediumship, which by contrast consists of the spiritual mind of the medium communicating directly with the mind of the spirit entity.

Chapter 13

SPIRIT EVIDENCE

Ways in which spirits show their presence

In their efforts to uplift and support us on the physical plane, spirits can interact with us in many ways, yet without us realising. We may attribute their subtle hints and pieces of evidence to our overactive imagination. They will typically put thoughts, and positive or negative feelings about something, suddenly into our head for guidance and inspiration, for example reminding us about things that we ought to consider doing or not doing. We can believe that the thoughts are our own, but they are not really.

In addition, to prove their presence near us, spirits can leave a "calling card" for us, at times when we are at our most receptive. It must be in the right place and at the right time for us to notice it. The more we look out for them, the more things we will notice! Equally, sheer belief in the spirit side of life heightens our sensitivity to the existence of spirit around us.

The incidence of scents, unusual little noises, white feathers and small coins are often cited as examples, as are orbs of light, whether pictured on still photographs or, more impressively, darting erratically across videos. In actual fact, on camera, without any input from the human mind which might, under the right circumstances, create rare complete materialisations, spirits would photograph as orbs of pure energy.

You can see spirit as shadows, where the difference between light and dark is merely a vibrational change. And they can cause one part of your body to feel unusually cold, as proof of their presence.

For no apparent external reason, a candle flame may jump or be blown out by spirit. Then a kiss by spirit is like hairs or a cobweb lightly brushing or tickling your face or body.

Through a power surge – a sudden, brief increase in electrical energy, spirit can manipulate lights and switch them on and off. The easiest ones for spirit to control are those "always-on" with dimmer switches to adjust the brightness of compatible dimmable bulbs.

I myself experience my right eye watering – unusually just on the outside, as an emotional reaction when my wife, mother or another loved one is close by and interacting with my own energy field on a physical level.

One of the easier methods spirits will generally use is scents which would be out-of-place in a particular environment. To bring memories back to us, it might be the trademark perfume worn by the person in spirit, or for instance a scent ranging from flowers, soap, dried herbs or mothballs to burning candles or tobacco, newly mown grass, wood smoke or musty antique books. Our problem can lie in recalling from memory which spirit might be leaving which scent!

Physical objects moved by spirit energy

It can be far harder for spirits to move heavy objects, or say stop a clock or watch regularly at a certain time or open a door, even by combining collective energy and tapping into energy emanating from humans in the room. Nevertheless physical phenomena seem easier for spirit to produce in the presence of children, who generally radiate energy to excess.

Having said that, you can experiment in your lounge at home with untethered helium party balloons which, because of their lightness, spirit energy can manipulate and move from room to room, most easily when a balloon has partially deflated.

Here is a good visual example of such balloon movement from spirit activity as uploaded to YouTube:

https://youtu.be/pF0kt_4o8Mw

Another good experiment is to place a table tennis ball on a bed of talcum powder spread over a sheet of dark paper, so as to trace how spirit can move the ball.

I have myself also witnessed how spirit energy can switch on the TV without anyone touching the remote. What is more, my wife Pam is well able to turn kitchen taps on and off, switch on a music CD player, or relocate small objects (aka "apports") such as would fit into the palm of your hand. To facilitate apports, spirit changes the vibrational frequency of the atoms comprising an object.

In my experience they have included keys and an empty red wristwatch box, not to mention an old pocket diary of Pam's which disappeared and rematerialised several days later in a friend's apartment 40 miles away. Teleportation of the diary over such a distance would have required the residual energy of a dozen spirits working together. The purpose of that exercise by spirit was for Pam's friend to be able to read her diary.

Later in this Chapter, I detail one particular personal experience which illustrates the transference of apports. All such well-meant spirit activities take place without advance warning, and you come to accept them as normal occurrences.

Nonetheless in many cases, given our busy lives, we may fail to notice items which have been subtly moved around, such as clothes on a rail or objects along a shelf.

Channelling healing energy from the spirit world

Further proof of spirit interaction with us is the catalogue of successes achieved by energy healing therapies. When you perform spiritual healing (including more ritualistic techniques originally from the Far East such as Japanese reiki, Indian pranic healing and Chinese qigong), you serve as a channel for energy from the spirit world to carry out the actual healing. In contrast, with direct energy healing you employ your own energy, which naturally drains you far more.

Simple and safe, non-invasive spiritual healing aims to overcome the disconnect, or lack of synchronicity, between mind, body and spirit that gives rise to ill health, as well as to stimulate the body's own natural healing ability.

Accordingly, such healing seeks to treat the underlying cause rather than the pain itself, bringing comfort and reassurance and helping you accept more what is going on within your physical body, mind and spirit, bringing the three closer together. They interact with each other continuously.

Practitioners among mediums channel non-physical healing energy – either from combined spirit teams or from a single spirit at a higher vibration – that is present around a third party, person or animal requiring help. Mediums act as a conduit for vibrational healing energy to flow through: they do not speak, and their ego and personality play no part in the process at all.

Repeated sessions are going to be needed where a deep-seated illness may have built up steadily over years, and people often do not turn to spiritual healing until very late on, as a "last-chance saloon" when a health condition has already greatly deteriorated.

Incidentally, spiritual healing is completely non-denominational and quite different to faith healing based upon a religion. Healing energy can be transferred "hands on" to the individual, often making the healer's hands noticeably red and warm – or indeed at a distance of many miles with no diminution in its effectiveness.

The legacy of Harry Edwards

Founded in 1954, the National Federation of Spiritual Healers (NFSH), also known

Harry Edwards, 1893-1976
www.harryedwardshealingsanctuary.org.uk

since 2009 as the Healing Trust, is a registered British charity of some 6,500 members aiming to increase knowledge and understanding of the healing gift. The internationally renowned healer Harry Edwards was member no.1 of the NFSH and its President up to his passing in 1976.

An important development took place the following year, when the General Medical Council in England agreed to allow doctors to recommend spiritual healing to their patients.

The first healer actually on the payroll of the National Health Service, from 1999 to 2011, was reiki exponent Angie Buxton-King. She integrated spiritual energy channelling with conventional medical care at the University College London Hospital (UCLH), where she ran a team of complementary therapists in the haematology unit.

In memory of Angie's son Sam who passed aged 10 in 1998 with acute myeloid leukaemia involving abnormal white blood cell production, the Sam Buxton Sunflower Healing Trust charity has since 2006 been supporting cancer patients and their families by providing funds to employ complementary therapists in the NHS and at hospices.

In fact Harry Edwards's vision for the future was that of doctors and healers working alongside each other, and for healers to be available nationwide. Helping to facilitate this, the Harry Edwards Healing Sanctuary in Surrey, UK, has been providing spiritual healing and training with conspicuous success since he set it up in 1946.

The Harry Edwards Healing Sanctuary is located in the Burrows Lea country house, Shere, Surrey

Another notable organisation of global reach (40 countries in 20 languages) providing courses and workshops is the Brofman Foundation for the Advancement of Healing. It is located in French-speaking Geneva and based upon the healing principles adduced by the former Wall Street computer expert Dr Martin Brofman (1940-2014), when he cured himself of a terminal cancer of the spinal cord in 1975.

Experiments to bring spirits forward

A number of basic experiments, when conducted correctly and accurately, can demonstrate the presence of spirits by using participants' energies, and each is arguably a science in its own right.

Tests include table tilting, glass divination and using a pendulum or dowsing rods over a board marked in segments, with spirits indicating "Yes", "No" or "I don't know" in response to your questions. Spirit boards, with a planchette using the light, unguided pressure of a fingertip, can facilitate automatic writing.

Such experiments can prove to people without a medium's input what spirit activity is present around them. Each participant should best have a quietened, clear, innocent and open mind and not be desperate for a message. One or more disbelievers or out-and-out sceptics can upset the whole exercise by harbouring low expectations and negative energy.

Glass divination

In for example glass divination, spirit can move an upturned tumbler around a table by using the energies of people seated around it. Each member of a group of say four to six people around the table rests the tip of their index finger lightly on the top of the tumbler, which will move in a given direction for "Yes" and elsewhere for "No" or "Maybe".

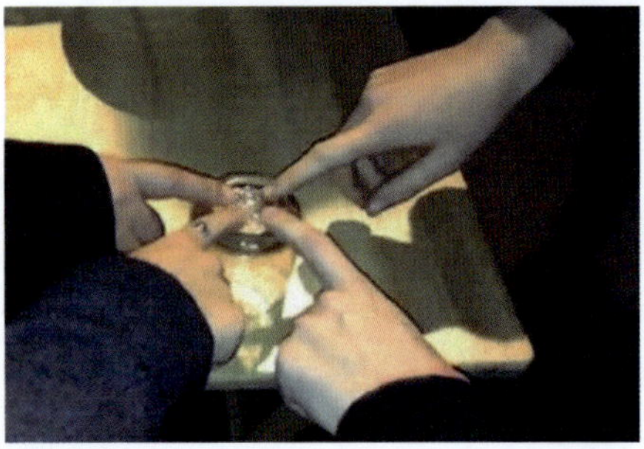

Example of glass divination with fingertips resting on an upturned tumbler

To confirm an active presence in this experiment, the motion is circular, and you can request the spirit to reverse the direction of travel as part of the exercise. Initially the spirit is asked to move the glass towards the person with whom he or she prefers to communicate.

You need to get the glass moving around circularly before putting each question, and the preferred communicator might initially ask, out loud or in his or her mind: "Are you a man?", "Are you a woman", "Are you a member of my family?", "Are you a friend of mine?" Spirit can move the glass at different speeds too, whilst a fresh person coming onto the table in place of another will change the energy and the experience.

Teamwork between people & spirits

In their role of watching over their nearest and dearest on earth, spirits have empathy and sympathy with us when we suffer anxiety and pain, not just affording us mental support, but also changing things out of the blue in our physical world to benefit us. Spirits can and do help us in many ways, often unseen.

Taking this to a higher level, I have encountered at first hand some astonishing examples of physical teamwork between spiritually aware people and their family spirits to achieve a common goal. Working as a team, you can achieve much more than you ever would as lone operators.

However, despite having a superior intellectual energy and knowing a lot more about us and our future than we do ourselves, spirits are barred from dictating our actions. We are free to accept or ignore any advice they may give. The reason for this is that the whole point of living a physical life is to make our own choices and mistakes and learn from that, to learn from hardships and challenges and use all the experiential knowledge gained over a lifetime to improve the quality of our spirit within.

Yet we can always ask the spirit world for help when in a predicament. So below I give a simple example of spirit answering a minor "cry for help".

Teleportation of small objects

An object can be transferred from one place to another by spirits' activity, either to prove their presence – or to aid us where we are very anxious about something. In spiritual terminology, the object moved is called an "apport".

The movement of subatomic particles described in quantum physics could be the principle by which apports convert to pure energy, to allow their transfer through space and time before they rematerialise, restored to their original physical state, in a different location.

This phenomenon cannot be dismissed out of hand, merely on the basis that it lies beyond the current level of scientific knowledge. I described back in Chapter 1 the standpoint of the Italian quantum physics theoretician Professor Carlo Rovelli that science should be a continuous process of challenging the validity of accepted knowledge and exploring new avenues of research.

So I experienced an apport for the first time when I was in a panic, having thought I had lost my electronic car key on a dog walk in heavy snow near my home.

My late wife and mother picked up on my appeal for help. They used teamwork to combine their own energies with other available spirit energies, possibly including even my own – and transported the missing key to where I could find it. Accordingly I suddenly saw it on my hall carpet, which had been double-checked and verified several times before as being completely clear. At a later sitting they admitted doing this.

A sufficient build-up of energy levels in a room can facilitate the teleportation of small objects, as well as lifting far heavier items, generally tables, off the ground.

A simple experiment I do before I go to bed at night is to give my mind a proper rest, clearing it of chatter and clutter, and meditate by focussing on a lighted candle with relaxing background music. Family spirits will then try to interact with my individual senses to prove their presence. That attempted interaction might consist of a recognisable perfume or aroma from the past, a touch on the skin or hair, or a particular emotion coming out of the blue.

So those were some of my experiences, and I am now looking forward to many more in the future.

Spirit interaction with our minds

Through orderly planning, collective spirit energies can be marshalled, moved about and metaphorically speaking "bent around corners": thereby traditional science as we know it goes right out of the window.

Nevertheless, in most circumstances it is easier for spirits to interact with us not physically but via our minds, putting unexpected thoughts into our brain which we regard as arising spontaneously, as mentioned earlier. In December 2018 my mother helpfully tipped me off by thought that the local motorbike cop in a North Wales village was concealed in bushes around the next bend, just the other side of a 30mph sign, brandishing his hand-held radar speed gun!

In some cases I have studied, the mind of a third party can certainly be influenced by spirit to make a decision in your favour. The scenario is common enough of a person-to-person interview, test or assessment where the interviewer, examiner or other decisionmaker needs to make a subjective final judgement in his or her mind as to the performance and credibility of the person in the hot seat opposite?

More detailed messages will typically come to us when we are in a dream or daydreaming state, or in that familiar no-man's-land emerging from sleep or dozing.

Daydreaming is the stream of consciousness that detaches from current external tasks, when attention drifts in a more personal and internal direction. People who daydream, thereby using their uncommon mind and letting go of the common mind, tend to have more experiences of spirit than those who do not daydream.

Chapter 14

REINCARNATION & THE LEARNING OF LESSONS

Birth, reincarnation & coming home to spirit

The spirit guides Alfred and Edward have divulged to us the really interesting fact that up to 10% of spirits who communicate through mediums have never actually been in a womb and chosen to have a physical life and become a soul within a body. One might add that the multitudes of spirits who have walked the earth in long-gone human epochs are of course unlikely to find any appropriate, physical family members with whom to communicate in the 21st century!

From the above statistic we might deduce that some 10% of the totality of many millions of spirits have never undertaken a physical existence in order to learn lessons through facing experiences. However, for the rest, the soul may be said to acquire its individuality via a life in a physical body on the earth plane.

Existing on a different, higher vibration, spirit is always spirit, even when encased in a human body as a soul and experiencing the physical life mapped out for it in the here-and-now. Spirit knows that it will always survive and will ultimately return to the community of the spirit world, its true home.

Co-existence of one soul in two worlds

Nevertheless, whilst undergoing a new physical life in earthly form, a soul can still communicate with us spirit-to-spirit via an all-knowing, higher part of its consciousness which is perpetually anchored in the spirit world.

That route for communication is the one taken by the spirit guide Edward, in order to find out about my own previous lives, for example, and be able to report that information through his trance medium.

This co-existence of one soul in two worlds on two different vibrations, higher and lower, is yet another difficult reality for us to take on board.

Then, when souls return to their real home in spirit, they re-engage with their individual higher spirit consciousness permanently resident there – with its store of knowledge and wisdom gathered from past life experiences.

Assuming a temporary identity

A human life is much like a part in a play. You assume a temporary identity just for the duration of the play and then go back to your normal, natural home in spirit after your performance has ended. This notion was never better expressed than by William Shakespeare in Act II of "As You Like It":

"All the world's a stage,
And all the men and women merely players;
They have their exits and their entrances,
And one man in his time plays many parts,
His acts being seven ages . . . "

But equally there is reincarnation – a whole new life in the physical dimension for an existing soul.

You glimpse their soul history when choosing your parents

Some souls may wish to reincarnate soon after death, whilst others decide to be reborn every century or several centuries.

It goes without saying that any new life has to be in the human future and cannot be in the past, which would be physically impossible. It may be comforting to those contemplating future lives to know that a host of deadly diseases have now been conquered, and yet different perils and challenges exist worldwide in the 21st century which were unknown to previous generations!

You have a short decision time to choose your own parents and life from a limited few put in front of you. However you are free to change your mind and can at that stage say "No" to embarking on any proposed new life.

Crucially, to make your all-important selection, you only get a glimpse of the souls of your prospective parents and nothing of their physical selves.

In this brief look from the spirit vibration you inhabit, you see the complete soul as it is with a compilation of all of its historical lives (a bit like simultaneous video conferencing images), its accumulated experience and the struggles it has undergone, but not the reasons why.

You are aware of certain things you will need to achieve in the course of your new physical life, yet do not know how they will actually come about.

You get very little information about the new life. Human characteristics such as gender, nationality, ethnicity and health condition are not on the table for selection. Furthermore you are not shown how long each life will last: learning is the key, and you may learn far more in a brief life of eight years than in one lasting 80.

Synchronising all the elements of your new life

At the outset, the choices are worked out for you, based upon the coincidence of time and place, how much you can learn and achieve, and how you would interact with and enrich the lives of contemporaneous people and spirits.

How all of these diverse elements can possibly harmonise is far from obvious to us. We are reminded here of the thinking of the Swiss analytical psychologist Carl Jung in the first half of the 20th century.

Jung used the term synchronicity to delineate events as "meaningful coincidences" if they occur with no apparent causal relationship and yet are meaningfully related. In line with that, events connected by meaning need to have no explanation in terms of cause-and-effect.

With the benefit of insight and perspective, we might come to the rational conclusion that coincidences are not random at all, but in fact a preordained concurrence of events or circumstances, intended all the way along by a higher authority, the boundless intellect of spirit. There is reasoning behind everything that happens in a life, and it is all integrated and coordinated.

Our future choices are known in advance

Yet this does not deny us our freewill nor prevent us from making our own independent judgements and decisions as part and parcel of synchronicity. We carry personal responsibility for our own actions on earth. However, as hard as it is for us to grasp, it just means that our future choices are known in advance to the spirit world, where man-made linear time does not exist, and therefore everything is happening in the present.

The nature and established behaviour patterns of an individual should in theory govern how he or she will respond to a given set of circumstances arising in their life, so that their actions and reactions can often be accurately predicted on that basis.

Nevertheless chance events can always intrude to muddy the water and bring about changes in the decisions and measures taken. Yet those unexpected events and their outcomes are already mapped out in advance and known in the timeless spirit world.

So, to sum up, once you have chosen to enter the physical world, you know that the intellect of spirit will synchronise the totality of time, place and objectives, not to mention future interrelationships and interactions, like a complex military operation.

That supreme intellect places before you the best possible choices for you to learn the required lessons and to feed and advance your soul by means of your experiences. It will then be up to you whether you take the right paths or not.

Life begins at conception

You make your final selection prior to conception, so that the spirit resides within a human baby throughout its nine months in the womb and equally in the case of a miscarriage or an abortion.

Extraordinarily, an experienced lady medium from North Wales whom I interviewed for this book has communicated via a third party medium with the spirit of her aborted son. Sometime after his own passing, the medium's late husband came through, bringing with him the child whom he named as Peter. From spirit, Peter wished mainly to reassure and comfort his mother, whilst not having much experiential memory to share, given that his physical life had been very brief.

There is continuing interaction between the mother's spirit and the embryo's spirit within the womb. The fact that life begins at conception in this way gives a huge boost of course to the arguments of pro-life campaigners.

So the spirit world knows in advance whether twins, triplets or other multiple births will take place, with one spirit predetermined per child.

Reincarnation in the physical world has to be in a future earth time. You can never interfere with a family tree nor go back in time to rewrite history.

The medium's mind works at different depths

The spirit guide Alfred volunteered to work with Robin, as an experiment from the commencement of his mediumship, despite not having worked with a medium before. Nevertheless Alfred synchronises well, every time he comes through, with the vibration level of Robin's mind.

He introduces new thoughts and ideas periodically into his mind to help him along, for example topical themes for Robin's platform addresses. One of Alfred's wider objectives is to encourage Robin at some point in the future to progress from evidential to trance mediumship, taking his mind to a far greater depth.

Speaking of which, a medium's depths of working vary widely – from easy, relaxed banter with a typical family spirit at a platform demonstration to communication with spirit guides on high vibration levels and up to trance mediumship and more.

Evolution of the composite consciousness

And so, in his high vibration conversations with Robin, Alfred admits to having had four lives in total, three male preceded by a far tougher first life from a physical point of view as a female. For ease of identification, we always work with one persona of his, Alfred the Victorian era undertaker as described in the next Chapter.

Yet the communicator from the spirit world whom we call Alfred is in reality a "composite consciousness", combining the knowledge, experience and memories accrued from all of the lives he has led.

Alfred explains to us that every reincarnated soul or spirit returns to the physical plane to be reborn as human or animal, male or female, in whatever country, in order to survive trials and tribulations, gain new experiences, and learn important lessons which will assist the evolvement, education and enlightenment of that spirit. Those lessons may include ongoing ones unfulfilled and therefore carried over from previous lives.

Lifeplan of lessons for soul progression

It's all about the progression of the spiritual energy from life to life, in whatever lifeform it needs to learn the appropriate lessons and feed off the experiences which will help that soul to become a stronger force. What is more, the parents of a newborn baby are also meant to learn lessons from the experience.

You do not select your own form, gender, race or nationality for reincarnation: the lessons that you need to learn are the key determinant and are a "committee decision" made by your soul group, your spirit family, with all their accumulated wisdom.

What is sometimes termed your "soul contract", framed in advance of conception and birth, is essentially the lifeplan of principal lessons that you and those around you are meant to learn over your new lifetime, in order to advance your soul and theirs to a higher level of consciousness. That hit-list may well include goals in terms of experiences not achieved as they should have been in previous lifetimes.

In a life where a child dies young, bearing in mind that infant mortality used to be a common occurrence, there is often a "soul contract" in place whereby the soul agrees to die young so that his parents can learn particular life lessons through pulling on their emotions. A short life is not a punishment but a learning opportunity, albeit a difficult lesson for all to learn.

Deciding to undertake a physical life

Birth and rebirth, natural evolvements for the spiritual being within us, are always our decision of "if and when". There is no set time for this: two centuries or two months can equally occur between successive lives. But, to restate the key point made above, you cannot choose your new gender, ethnicity or nationality.

Some spirits choose not to come back and prefer to experience only one life in human form, given all its traumas, sufferings and hardships. And to undergo a physical life, they are also obliged to painfully leave all their loved ones behind in the spirit world, which constitutes their real home. By contrast, other souls may wish to undergo ten or more lives in different cultures over centuries, to learn hugely from them, feeding off experiences and getting ever stronger.

Returning to the spirit world, we need an interval to adjust to and accept the spirit life, process what we have learned on earth in the last life and thereby advance in spirit. On our return, our strongest memories are going to be of our immediate past life, but we also have recollections of every previous life that we have lived. We need to know all the lessons we have learned from previous lives!

A greater period may possibly be spent in the spirit world assimilating an abundance of lessons where the past life has been a long and full one, and thus any reincarnation would be later. That being the case, the spirit of a small child with minimal lifespan and experiences might be offered a far quicker reincarnation.

Advancement through reincarnation

You can return – although not necessarily in the next life, a completely different one of course, but maybe in a later life than that – in order to best learn a lesson not properly mastered by you the first time around, or to teach other people their lessons, or both ways. Everything is part of a learning curve!

Reincarnation mirrors the Buddhist doctrine of rebirth or metempsychosis – the passing of the soul or spirit at a particular physical death into another body, human or animal, male or female. Whatever body is chosen, it is no more than an outer form or shell to host the spirit which itself has an eternal life.

Additionally, the simplicity, benevolence and fundamental respect for all living things integral to the Buddhist faith are the closest to such fundamental characteristics of the spirit world as "oneness", the equitable sharing of resources and the desire to improve the lives of others regardless of personal gain.

Even the historical "seven principles of spiritualism as a religion", as detailed at the end of Chapter 11, may be said to fall down on the fact that they relate purely to the individual and not to the individual's interaction and relationship with other people or living things.

Put in simple terms by the spirit guide Edward, the life force of God moves through every living being, and you can indeed choose to be reincarnated as a humble animal. Sometimes we cannot learn lessons appropriately in human form and so must experience life as another species.

Your chosen host for reincarnation aims to maximise the value from a spiritual point-of-view that lies within the experience, and within even the worst experiences is the opportunity for advancement, as Edward makes clear. All experience is a process of personal education.

Learning from human experience

Instead of moving on through the spiritual spheres, souls, having freewill, can choose to come back to the earth plane to be schooled in new experiences and share them with others: it is always their individual choice. Some learning can only be successfully achieved by the mind within a physical body.

The soul often comes back because it feels it has unfinished business here, but always to learn lessons, choosing a new physical form with the right circumstances it requires in order to learn them. There is no point in coming back as a monk if, to learn lessons, you need to live the life of a hoodlum!

The next life chosen might be to reassess the learning of those lessons, go more in-depth with them, revisit them if not taken in properly the first time, or move on to new lessons. What is more, setbacks can occur in a life, say through our thirst for money, power or fame, which do not advance our process of learning but actually set it back!

Foreknowledge would be self-defeating

The new persona is separate to the spirit and always supersedes the previous persona, much like a re-recording over a tape, although some deep-seated personality traits will remain.

Neither personae nor souls on earth know the reasons why they have come to earth until they return to their real home in spirit – and re-engage with their individual higher spirit consciousness permanently resident there with all the knowledge and wisdom archived from their past life experiences.

Otherwise, burdened with that knowledge, they might overanalyse everything they do and be too self-critical, instead of just getting on with their new life and being the person they need to be. If they knew in advance what they were supposed to do, this would most likely affect their life choices, depressing their motivation and psyche, and they might not follow the path mapped out for them.

If you knew that you would become the champion in a sport whatever you did, would you apply as much effort to it? Then, if you were aware of your failings in a previous life, next time you would avoid them and thereby be driven by fear rather than natural instinct. In a similar vein, religions can arguably in some cases make you do good from fear not inner conviction.

Our mind reigns supreme and has the main say in our life choices, not the body nor the spirit within us. Having said that, serious addictions and compulsions can allow the body to overpower the mind. In the end we are all here to make our mistakes and learn from them.

"Catch-22" paradoxes

This is a self-defeating paradox, a "Catch-22" as illustrated by Joseph Heller's 1961 satirical novel and Mike Nichols's 1970 Paramount Pictures feature film of that name.

The book and film refer to a supposed rule applied to a US Air Force squadron stationed on a Mediterranean island off Italy during World War 2 whereby bomber pilots continuing to fly dangerous combat missions without asking to be relieved are regarded as mental. However, if they have the good sense to make such a request, that very act shows that they are sound enough mentally to continue flying and makes them ineligible to be relieved.

Hence "Catch-22" is defined as a problematic situation or challenge for which the only solution is denied by a circumstance inherent in it.

Everyday examples abound. If you lose your glasses, in order to be able to look for them you need to find them first. Or you cannot call to report a fault on your landline because the line is not working. You need to have experience to get a job, but you need a job to get experience. To get a job, you need a car, but to afford a car, you need a job. You cannot get an appointment with your doctor because he or she is off ill. And so "Catch-22" paradoxes are not uncommon in life.

In a similar vein, foreknowledge or prescience would hardly work as a long-term development or problem-solving exercise for souls on earth and also, as soon as they had done the minimum necessary, they might want to return to spirit.

Our journey through the physical life is just not like that in practice and is always regarded by us as a new opportunity. Furthermore, however much we think that we are in control of our lives, we continually have to react to chains of external events in motion above and beyond us.

Lessons learned can take many forms

In all cases, the lessons assimilated from its physical experiences go back with the soul to the spirit world, enriching both that soul and the spirit world as a whole. What choices do we make, and how do we react to the many different challenges that we may face in life?

We cannot really know what extreme hunger, thirst, poverty, disability, bereavement or any other form of suffering is like, or talk about it authoritatively, unless we have experienced it. That makes sense, doesn't it? Accordingly the worst ordeals can offer the best opportunities for spiritual progression.

Some lessons can be learned in a few moments of our lives, others can take a lifetime to learn. Some we do not learn but have to revisit time and again in the same life – or in a future one, as per the example below citing Miss Evelyn Lovick.

What the human mind strives for can take us away from our spiritual goals and lessons, and then a conflict may arise between earthly and spiritual learnings. Thus it can be a question not of what pinnacle you attain (say in education, arts and sciences, business or sport), but how you attain it and handle the recognition.

Lessons learned can take many forms. Maybe they relate to making the most of what you've got, counting your blessings, or keeping a cool head in a manic and hazardous world? Or making decisions for yourself rather than following others. Perhaps lessons will involve controlling your emotions, discovering the true meaning of love, or growing out of childish things and "acting your age".

Schooling can be in adopting the principles of morality and duty towards others, or showing empathy, kindness and generosity towards them, particularly your enemies? Can we learn to understand why they have done what they have done to us? Tolerance, forgiveness and acceptance tend to be the most difficult things for us humans to learn.

If they are very family-orientated, reincarnated souls may need to live without having relatives, to learn the lesson of personal survival with no family support, or cope with the trauma of losing parents or children. Others might feel guilty about once killing an animal for pleasure and never want to do that again. Souls might learn from having a lottery windfall and then squandering it all.

A suicide may be part of the journey, not only as an experience but also to witness the pain that it inflicts on those left behind and how loved ones cope after the passing. With any bereavement, lessons are learned by both parties to the experience, the deceased and the bereaved.

Revisiting lessons & switching roles in a future life

We have spoken about revisiting lessons in a future physical life, and how events significant to the individual will impact other people around and yet be felt differently by each person involved.

As an illustration, an unmarried mother might undergo the traumatic experience of having to permanently let go of her baby son to adoptive parents and live with that. This is exactly what happened to the late Miss Evelyn Lovick, who was the resident housekeeper for two of my uncles in Manor Road, Solihull, West Midlands from the 1960s through most of the 1980s.

In a sitting on 7th January 2020, Evelyn came through to explain to Robin and myself how this works. By choosing that lesson again in a future existence, her spirit could switch roles and reside within a different player in a similar scenario, for example the father of the child, to see the experience of the son's life from a different angle. Or next time, as the mother again, she might keep the child and not give him up for adoption. Or her child might die early. Or her spirit could reside within the child itself.

Chapter 15

PAST LIVES & PAST LIFE MEMORIES

Different lives & personae for the same soul

If the soul is say of a particularly caring, sensitive or healing nature, then it is always likely to be so in whichever life it may choose to embark upon. Personality traits and physical characteristics will, more often than not, live on in successive personae.

Aspects of past lives can also filter through to us as "déjà-vu", the feeling of an intense familiarity we cannot understand with a circumstance, landscape, person or place that we have never seen before.

Déjà-vu is encountered by adults and children alike, and any of our five senses can trigger the sensation. It occurs regularly in dream states too, or transfers from dreams to reality in the waking state. An alternative explanation is that the "timeless" spirit world may give us an inkling of a life experience which, for them, is not in the past but being played out in the here-and-now.

The same soul can undergo numerous reincarnations and experiences, so that mere physical appearance at any one time is deceptive. It is like a suit of clothes or a cocoon that you can cast off. Arguably the spirits of the most reviled figures of the 20th century such as Hitler, Stalin and Pol Pot could easily have moved on to their next lives in the 21st century.

What is more, by enriching life experience through lessons learnt, previous existences can build up understanding and enable a soul to advance to a higher level of vibration or enlightenment.

Of these, the last life undergone is generally the most prominent. As mentioned earlier, the soul, the consciousness, in the spirit dimension tends to project the individuality, memories and concerns of its immediate past life and likes to relate that experience to current happenings, such as family business, on the physical plane.

What is more, the persona of the spirit's last life chronologically is usually – but not always – going to be the most identifiable and recognisable one for communicating with relatives and friends remaining on earth.

Knowledge of past lives in our higher spirit consciousness

Meanwhile, if we undertake "past lives regression" through hypnosis, then it will take us back through time to the collective souls of our past. Because our higher spirit consciousness stores the knowledge of all our previous lives and personalities, these can be unlocked from history as past life memories.

An expert researcher in this field was the Californian hypnotherapist Dr Michael Newton (1931-2016). He developed his own regression technique and founded the Newton Institute to establish a global training network for it, now spanning 26 countries.

Equally, any spirit or spirit guide in their world can go deep enough to glimpse, and share information on, the multiple lives stored in another spirit's higher consciousness in a way that a regular evidential medium cannot. The ability to view and interrogate a composite spirit on all its levels is quite different to a medium's skill in communicating with the consciousness of that spirit's last life in time order.

Nevertheless, depending on their way of working, some evidential and trance mediums can engage their spirit guides to obtain any past life information from another spirit's higher consciousness permanently resident in the spirit world.

Previous lives are like an open book

As energies are transferred between spirits, then they easily learn about each other and share their most enduring memories from past lives. Within the group consciousness or group knowledge, the entire history of a spirit's previous lives is like an open book to other spirits – there is no secrecy.

My late wife Pam described this as "having a simultaneous awareness of multiple TV or CCTV screens – in the eternal Now" for viewing memories recollected by another spirit from its multiple previous lives.

A physical representation – as a video wall of CCTV displays – of ambient spirits' past life memories in the eternal "Now"

Yet you cannot tell from those views whether a given spirit was resident in an animal or human form. The view that my wife most understands will be to the fore, possibly showing a life where she may have interacted with the other spirit as a family member, friend or pet animal.

The group consciousness as a diamond of countless facets

A massive diamond with an infinite number of facets is a common way of depicting the group consciousness, the "oneness", showing the lives of individual spirits as separate facets, cheek by jowl and in constant interaction with one another.

A spirit's immediate past life is usually the most important facet to bring forward and talk about, because it describes the most recognisable and provable experiences and interactions with people on the earth plane.

Experiences from other lives, going back perhaps hundreds of years in history, are simultaneously recollected on other facets of the diamond, less prominent and yet still as fresh and clear as if they had occurred yesterday. Changing the analogy slightly, when you roll a dice, the face which ends up on top – as your latest previous life – means that others of equal weight are heeded less.

There again, how natural white light separates into its constituent colours becomes evident when a beam enters a triangular prism. The device disperses that white light into violet, indigo, blue, green, yellow, orange and red, a rainbow effect of multiple colours of different wavelengths (as illustrated in Chapter 3).

In a similar fashion, the memories of multiple past lives become evident to all spirits on returning home to the spirit world from the physical body and re-engaging with their particular higher spirit consciousness permanently resident in that world.

My wife's previous lives

Fortunately the spirit guide Edward was able to give me information as below about my late wife's three principal previous existences before she was Pam. This serves to demonstrate the longevity, and indeed the eternal nature, of spirit, as well as how common characteristics can run like a thread through different lives over centuries.

As Edward first revealed and Pam herself has confirmed in sittings, in her first life almost 2000 years before, a facet of my wife's spirit now was embodied in a female warrior in western Egypt called, phonetically, Sinvi.

She was fixated on washing, cleanliness and water and owned a number of horses. This incarnation was a commanding figure, riding a chariot and carrying a spear, who had been in battle more than once. In that epoch, warfare purely for survival was far from being an adult male preserve, and even children were expected to fight. Nevertheless, when growing up, Sinvi had also tended livestock such as lambs and goats and the family vineyards for wine production.

Much later Pam had been Charlotte, the hard-working daughter of a poor white woodsman outside Lyon, France: she passed there at 15 years of age in 1745 from an epidemic, a fever, moving through that part of France at the time. One of her many chores for the family was to draw water from a fast and fiercely flowing

My wife Pam, 1955-2014, relaxing by the sea front at New Quay, Pembrokeshire, West Wales, on 22nd June 2009

Pam at Alderley Edge, Cheshire, on Monday 23rd June 2008, en route to celebrating our silver 25th wedding anniversary that week in Brontë country

stream. Her duties also included work and interaction with animals like horses and even killing chickens to put food on the table.

Thirdly she had lived as a black male called Jinobee, brother of the chieftain of a small, peace-loving tribe totalling 60 or so in a village in southern Africa, leading a native and very primitive life surrounded by children and animals.

Food, water and sheer survival were their principal concerns. Yet, at 40 years of age, Jinobee was mortally wounded in the chest with his own spear whilst on the ground, in a scuffle between his tribe and British colonial troops in August 1883 after the first Boer War.

Apart from anything else, from a philosophical perspective, such examples of changing personae show just how senseless and absurd are the conflict and discrimination which we have always experienced in our earthly society between men and women, racial types, nationalities and skin colours.

And so my wife's fondness for the countryside, fear of fast-running water (from one particularly threatening experience in her existence by Lyon, as described above, when small) and the common denominator in her various lives – a close affinity with animals – lived on in her soul during our married life between 1983 and her passing in 2014. Nevertheless she had no qualms about going on trips in small boats or wading through the surf!

Incidentally, many other common yet debilitating phobias, such as a fear of heights, agoraphobia, astraphobia, cynophobia or haemophobia, are known to live on from a person's previous lives. Within the personality or psychological blueprint of any individual will be traits from their past existences.

My own previous existences

By quizzing my higher spirit consciousness dwelling in his world, the spirit guide Edward has uncovered some details of my own previous lives.

So I was an orphan, homeless, starving and desolate, called Richard O'Connolly, who during the 18th century lived in a large, old building that served as a refuge or shelter for waifs and strays, in Kings Street, central Dublin. I toiled in the local government, not private, workhouse and returned to spirit at the age of only 12, succumbing to a combination of diseases including tuberculosis. My sister Mary died at an equally young age.

Around 1750 I was then a career parliamentarian in London called William Morse. As such, I was even a confidant of a female member of the British Royal family under George II, and yet I died young.

In contrast, Edward says that my next life was as Pierre, a once affluent Frenchman who ran an export-import shipping business near a French port. My unfortunate demise was barely noticed amongst the many thousands of deaths around the Terror period of the French Revolution in 1793-94. I had lost most of my money through poor business decisions and, although apparently happily married, had an illicit affair with a titled married lady which brought about my execution arranged by her influential husband.

Next I was an early Victorian sheep farmer called Thomas Webb on a remote farm in the Great Yarmouth area of the Norfolk Broads. I lived with my wife (our children having left home) and passed at 62 years of age from pneumonia.

My mother lived one previous life – as a man

Coincidentally sharing the same birthday as him, March 10th, my mother had had only one previous life, as Charles Edwards from a wealthy English landowning family living in a rural Essex mansion in Victorian times. Charles was the middle child of five. The two eldest were daughters, and he was the oldest of three following sons.

However, mixing metaphors, he kicked over the traces and was the black sheep of the family, so that his severe, Bible-punching father Peter obliged him to emigrate to seek out a new life and "make him stand on his own feet". Strict Christianity was deep-rooted in the family, since Peter's father had been a preacher and overseer of his own church in Cornwall.

Accordingly, in 1881 in his early 20s, Charles Edwards had to pay his own passage on a sailing vessel called "The Victor" from Portsmouth to New York, in the company of many Irish families eager for a fresh life and opportunities in the New World. A strong community spirit and close friendships developed amid difficult conditions on the ship.

Charles befriended an Irish lady four years older than him called Mary, whom he later went on to marry. The arduous six-week voyage was blighted by poor food and sanitation, which had led to numerous deaths among the migrants, including that of Mary's husband Declan.

As second-generation settlers, Charles and Mary travelled on very bad roads to a country area 35 miles from Washington DC, where Charles had a friend and bought land for farming cattle and poultry to live on. The homesteaders had made their choice, and there was never any prospect of going back. It was a far harder and tougher existence than Charles had ever imagined, since rustling and gun law were rife. It was a harsh, dog-eat-dog life, and you could trust nobody.

Later he opened a shop selling clothes and fabrics, a trade followed by his son Thomas, who went on to run a similar clothing retail business. But his other son William was a fiery-tempered rascal who wasted money and was jealous of Thomas's success, hence the two sons did not get on at all well with each other. They had a sister Mary, so there were three children in total.

Charles eventually passed to spirit in his 70s, having also been active in local American politics to help society based upon his Catholic convictions. His son Thomas became well-known too on the local political scene, which was dominated in that era by small, vociferous groups and rowdy meetings!

My father's three previous male lives

In contrast, my father had had three previous male existences. Firstly as a Roman foot soldier, Perseus, who died from a chest wound inflicted by native Greeks in battle outside a fort on one of their islands. Secondly as an impoverished and poorly nourished sheep farmer, Thomas Applebury, near Eastbourne, Sussex, in the mid-1700s.

Thirdly he was Black Tom, one of many notorious highwaymen and housebreakers who operated in farming country along the River Thames in London by Putney and Richmond around 1800.

Masked and with a choice of horses and saddle, Black Tom was black both of character and of temper. He used to hold up coaches, at times with associates, and to drink at (what was then) the Orange Tree Inn at Putney and other hostelries where he could sell or trade his booty.

He was eventually caught and hung at 32 years of age, with his body left to rot in summary local justice meted out by the wealthy landowning elite, in order to protect their own assets and give a stark warning to the mass of have-nots.

Extraordinarily, in Great Britain of those days, theft and debt were treated as far more heinous offences than manslaughter or crimes of violence. Moreover the first police force to patrol the streets of London, the Peelers, were not introduced until September 1829 by the criminal justice and prisons reformer Sir Robert Peel.

The common trait running through my father's lives was his will to survive or, latterly in the persona I knew, to win in competitive sports. Coincidentally, in all of his lives including that as my father, he had suffered severe health problems with his feet.

The other lives of spirit guide Alfred Quinn

Alfred has described his four lives to us in some detail. As a homeless girl in England in the 1500s given the name of Sheila, she had very little food and had to steal it and do odd jobs in order to survive and was also mistreated by people around her. She passed four months before her 17th birthday with a pneumonia-type disease and was buried in an unmarked grave.

Next, in the 1800s, Alfred was a highly respected undertaker (when he bore the name Alfred Quinn) in a family funeral directors, hatters and tailoring business. His shop was located in the working class, built-up area of Bridge Street, Belfast, where the local children used to play outside in bare feet. His mother had taught him how to sew, stitch and mend clothes, whilst his father had schooled him in the undertaking trade, both having learned their skills in turn from their family forebears.

Brought up as a strict Christian in that existence, Alfred was very quick-minded, had a wife called Mary and left a son when he passed in 1857, in his fifties, from pulmonary tuberculosis aka consumption. (The great German bacteriologist Dr Robert Koch did not isolate the bacillus causing tuberculosis until 1882.)

Alfred prefers to portray himself in this undertaker persona since he feels that it is easier for Robin to recognise and accept: Robin is familiar with his energy. He appears very slim, not muscly, in the build, height 5ft 9in and smartly dressed either with stripy trousers or in a dinner suit with bow tie. He wears a monocle, uses a magnifier for reading and walks with a gentleman's cane which had belonged to his father, who had died only in his thirties. Alfred had also lost a sister who was only in her twenties.

The spirit guide Alfred in his persona as the Belfast undertaker Alfred Quinn, who passed with lung disease in 1857 in his fifties. The first sitting in which Alfred came through to us was on May 20th 2018.

His following life was again as a devoutly Christian male. It was in remote Italian countryside around the turn of the century, in a small monastery where he had been brought up from a babe in arms.

Having been born with a malformed hand and withered muscles in his left arm (fated to have little use in them throughout his life), he was an unwanted orphan who would have been left to die had he not been charitably taken in by the monks. He became a helper wearing a monk's garb and was given the name of Stefanelli.

The monastic community was at least self-sufficient in food, albeit plain and unvaried at times including home-produced tomatoes and bread, using a watermill on a river nearby for flour grinding. They fed travellers passing through and even shod their horses via a blacksmith, being remunerated for their work.

As Stefanelli, most of Alfred's time and effort was spent performing wide-ranging if simple and menial tasks – conveying messages; fetching and carrying with his good hand to assist cooks and candlemakers; looking after chickens and collecting their eggs; helping to grow fruit and vegetables and taking plant cuttings; carving wooden bowls on a wood-turning lathe with a foot treadle; and feeding soup to monks sick in bed.

He himself was to die there of a heart condition at the age of 43 in 1918, the Great War having barely touched this community, such was its remoteness and isolation. That life was succeeded by one in more modern times as a boy with a short lifespan, but about which we know very little.

All these examples of past lives illustrate the point made early in Chapter 2 that the energy of spirits is eternal and cannot decay or die. And gender, nationality, ethnicity and skin colour will contrast widely in different past lives over different centuries.

The most that I have uncovered myself for a single spirit with whom we have communicated have been ten lives. And obviously that particular spirit has acquired vast knowledge along the way and is still very much active, because ageing does not come into it.

Prof Ian Stevenson & his research into past life memories

There are many fascinating descriptions of reincarnation out there. One of the specialists studying the phenomenon has been Professor Ian Stevenson (1918-2007), a psychiatrist born in Montreal but naturalised American, who worked for the University of Virginia School of Medicine for 50 years. He was Chair of the

Professor Ian Stevenson, University of Virginia School of Medicine

Department of Psychiatry from 1957 to 1967, the Carlson Professor of Psychiatry from 1967 to 2001, and a Research Professor of Psychiatry from 2002.

He became internationally recognised for his research into reincarnation by discovering evidence suggesting that memories and physical injuries can be transferred from one lifetime to another. He travelled extensively over a period of 40 years, investigating 3,000 cases of children around the world who recalled having had past lives.

His meticulous research presented evidence that such children had unusual abilities, illnesses and phobias which could not be explained by either heredity or environment. Among the most interesting areas in his investigation was the discovery of birthmarks and birth defects corresponding to wounds from a previous lifetime.

Reincarnation of wartime German air gunner

One of Professor Stevenson's documented case studies widely reported in the UK and overseas media was that of Carl Edon, a schoolboy from the town of Middlesbrough, North Yorkshire. The boy recalled in great detail his past life and background as wartime German air gunner Heinrich Richter.

Richter's turret gun was positioned at the rear of the cockpit, behind the pilot of a Messerschmitt Bf-110 bomber escort, from a Luftwaffe unit based at Schiphol in the Netherlands. The plane crashed in a fireball near Middlesbrough on January 15th 1942 after colliding with a barrage balloon cable:

www.dailymail.co.uk/news/article-6296347/Was-Luftwaffe-pilot-reincarnated-boy-Middlesbrough.html?ito=email_share_article-bottom

Heinrich Richter and Carl Edon even bore some facial resemblance to each other
***Images by courtesy of* www.dailymail.co.uk**

Prof Jim Tucker & his subject James Leininger

The American Jim B Tucker, a renowned child psychiatrist and also a Professor in the University of Virginia School of Medicine, collaborated with Ian Stevenson for several years on his research project into children's past life memories and took over the work when he eventually retired. One theory for this phenomenon occurring in youngsters is the unalloyed innocence of their mind and its openness to spirit in early years, before the historical memories eventually dissipate or are swamped by other things in life.

One of Tucker's best known cases was that of James Madison Leininger, a young boy in Lafayette, Louisiana, who in year 2000 began having intense nightmares of a plane crash. James later described being a US pilot killed in action when his fighter was shot down by the Japanese during the Battle of Iwo Jima.

He gave details which included the name of an aircraft carrier (the USS Natoma Bay), the first and last name of a pilot friend who was on the ship with him (Jack

Larsen), and the island location and other specifics of the fatal crash.

His parents eventually discovered a close correlation between James Leininger's statements and the loss of a 21-year-old US Navy fighter pilot from Pennsylvania called James McCready Huston on March 3rd 1945 during the Iwo Jima operation. Pictured here in his uniform, Huston is now remembered on the Honolulu Memorial to the Missing, Hawaii.

Professor Jim Tucker, University of Virginia School of Medicine

Lieutenant James McCready Huston – US Navy fighter pilot

Chapter 16

SPIRIT GUIDES

What are spirit guides?

Throughout a physical life, from birth to death, every human being has around him or her at least one primary spirit guide – as a helper, mentor, gatekeeper or "invisible brother or sister". Such guides are spirits of a very high vibration, rich in experience from past lives, who volunteer for the job.

Normally they stay unnoticed in the background and interact with our resident spirit only if they need to. That would be to provide succour and strength if and when we suffer life crises such a serious health issue, close family bereavement, marriage break-up, bankruptcy or imprisonment, or when we are at risk of passing and making our transition.

For more sensitive individuals open to spirit communication and interaction, a guide can also act as a gatekeeper, authorising or denying access by those spirits possibly too strong and forceful for a fragile, vulnerable or infirm human body to bear without causing health problems.

Your main spirit guide is agreed before your birth, a persona available from history and best suited in terms of a life experience which will assist your soul's learning process within its physical form.

What is more, your own principal guide can stay with you and continue to help and support your development as a spirit being after you have transitioned to the spirit world. In fact, in that world, there are guides who themselves have guides, each of whom have their own guides to advise them, and so on in succession.

Providing spirit-to-spirit guidance over a lifetime

It is a question of experience rather than knowledge, because the same unlimited reservoir of knowledge is, as described in Chapter 2, accessible to all spirits. Respect for rich life experience which puts a spirit onto higher vibrations is a fundamental attribute of the spirit world.

Spirit-to-spirit contact with our guide provides worldly and spiritual guidance where possible and assists our evolvement through learning lessons from life's experiences. It is entirely our choice as to whether or not we accept the ideas which spirit puts into our human mind.

In truth there will always be debate as to how many of mankind's greatest discoveries, creations and inventions have been inspired by ideas from spirit in the first place. Seeds are sown in the mind of the individual, and, when they grow, this has a knock-on effect to inspire all the others who come afterwards, whether in that field or wider society.

Instead of choosing to progress in the spirit world itself or to reincarnate again to achieve a higher rate of progression and development that way, a soul may get the opportunity to become a spirit guide and support the spirit resident in a human being "off and on" from a contact point-of-view for the duration of his or her life or lives on earth.

Indeed, in differing guises the main guide or gatekeeper can occasionally stay with a given spirit throughout its various lives on earth over centuries.

The persona & outward appearance of main spirit guides

In common with all spirits, main guides can assume any appearance they wish to, at any age and in any clothes, from any past life of theirs. Their precise guise is flexible and will often fit in with the beliefs and expectations of their host, who is perhaps visualising a character who is old, wrinkly, very wise and historically important!

Overall, the role of main guides is to sustain and nurture the spirit within us, and the contributions they make to this will vary according to their differing backgrounds, epochs, histories and experiences.

Guides must have lived in a previous era and will have had close cultural and traditional connections with their spiritual self. That may typically have been as a tribal chief, Indian mystic or ascetic, Chinese sage, Old Testament prophet, Native American squaw, Arctic Inuit, Mongolian shaman or Tibetan monk.

They can also adopt the form of Native American spirit or power animals such as eagles, crows, horses, bison, elks, cougars and grizzly bears, whatever a person's mind will be most comfortable with or most readily accept from their cultural background.

Nevertheless people are more likely to interact with a primary spirit guide familiar to them on a mental rather than purely visual level.

Mentoring & skills for specific activities

Additionally, subsidiary guides can come into a person's energy field to provide specialised expertise and advice on a temporary or limited basis. That is until his or her interest in a given subject dwindles – or those guides are supplanted by others who come along with a more advanced understanding to support subsequent phases of learning.

Different subsidiary guides will come and go and do different jobs to help the same spirit until such time as they feel they are no longer required. From their own practical experience on the earth plane, they will provide mentoring and skills for specific activities, stages or roles in a person's life. The latter range typically from subjects such as healing, historical research, the visual arts and handicrafts to leadership, public speaking and teaching.

Artists, writers, poets and musicians down the ages have claimed that their creative work is inspired by an individual whom they refer to as their "muse", their spiritual mentor who puts ideas and solutions into their head. And if their muse should leave them for any reason, then they simply cannot continue that particular line of work.

Muse is a term with origins in nine goddesses of Greek mythology, daughters of Zeus. Their perceived role in the ancient world was to help and inspire people to compose poetry and prose, originate visual and performing arts, and so forth.

Wide-ranging examples of spirit guides

During her physical life, one of my wife Pam's two spirit guides appeared in her dreams in the guise of a young Native Indian squaw of the Shawnee tribe, in her early teens and of similar physique to Pam. Given the common name of White Eagle, she had an attractive rounded face, dusky complexion and long, dark, straight hair and wore a large animal skin over her shoulders. Her father was a traditional, trance spiritualist, shaman, a very tall man and brother of the tribal leader, her uncle.

Pam's other spirit guide, as described in Chapter 5, was a nomadic tribal leader in the Holy Land of the Old Testament.

As for myself, one of my own spirit guides is Heinrich (known locally as Henry) Klein, a preacher man from remote farming country in Upper Austria. He had emigrated with his family in the 1850s to form a new Quaker community of several hundred in Kansas which was based on wheat farming. There Henry had four or more children and maintained a strict minimalist lifestyle.

Along with their renowned pacifism, the Quakers were also motivated by benevolent concern for Native Americans and the opportunity of voting against slavery in this newly opened territory. Dressed in black with traditional brimmed hat and bible in hand, Henry the preacher was a respected elder of the community who wrote spiritual and religious works for his people. He reached 72 years of age.

Another spirit guide of mine is a native North American tribal leader, dark in complexion, from the Apache Geronimo's era in the 1800s. He is depicted as strong in body, bare-chested and wearing native dress. Living in a sparse landscape of open fields with very few dwellings, he needed to hunt wild animals with spear in hand to feed his family. Then he was forced by gun-toting white immigrants moving westward to make a long march and live with his tribe on an Indian reservation, where he suffered greatly and perished at 59 from malnourishment.

My father's main guide or gatekeeper was Pier, a French monk in a remote, isolated monastery on the edge of the French Alps in the 16th to 17th century. The order had very little interaction with the outside world. There he studied spiritual matters, the stars and planets, wrote spiritual books and passed in his late 80s. His eyesight had declined greatly in his latter years, which prevented him from reading and writing which he had loved to do.

Xinu, the itinerant sage from Imperial China

As a further example, Alfred's main guide over two of his lives, Sheila and Stefanelli (see Chapter 14), appears in the persona of an itinerant monk, sage and teacher called Xinu, from the mountains of 15th century Imperial China.

Coincidentally, Xinu is also a subsidiary guide of Robin's for healing, supporting him currently when anyone around the world may request distant healing. Spirit-to-spirit healing by its nature can travel seamlessly across time and distance. Mediums can either take themselves to that person via astral projection of their soul or spirit, as explained in Chapter 2, or just send healing energy at long range.

As it happens, including his persona as a monk, Xinu himself has had nine lives in total around the world so far, from being a girl in ancient Egypt, who died very young, to his last one as a male Arctic Eskimo in the 1700s who reached his mid-40s.

What is more, the spirits of distinguished individuals from history can choose to interact with several lives on the earth plane simultaneously, not on an exclusive basis at all. Thereby they are able to inspire and mentor humans with whom they share an affinity based upon common interests to exceed their natural talents.

Interacting with your own spirit guide

Spirit guides are here to help us on the earth plane to move along and be at the right place at the right time, so to speak. Some are keener to interact with our resident spirit than others, it's their choice, and it also depends on how far we resonate with and accept them.

We can successfully recognise their presence and interact with them, typically when we are asleep and more receptive in our dream state. Nevertheless it is always going to be easier for a past family member more conversant with our personal memories and day-to-day psychology to put an idea or emotion into our mind than can a spirit guide.

Spirit guides and healing guides are, as we have said above, of very high vibration, having usually amassed a great deal of knowledge, understanding and experience. That comes from varied past existences and from other spirits around them, not to mention from watching us, witnessing our lives and how we deal with the challenging circumstances and events around us day-by-day.

On that basis, spirit guides are also here to help themselves – as a way of acquiring further experience and learning from that. To develop their fund of knowledge, they choose or volunteer to visit us from the spirit world rather than reincarnate again in human form. Accordingly they more than welcome the opportunity for personal growth and advancement at the sittings of a trance medium through whom they can physically speak.

Chapter 17

IN CONCLUSION

The positive message that "Life Goes On"

In this layman's guide I have sought to separate fact from fiction and discuss some key aspects of spiritualism and the afterlife, without getting bogged down in statements of the more obscure, quasi-religious terminology and philosophy you can encounter in spiritualism.

My overwhelmingly positive message to you, the reader, is that "Life Goes On" as soon as our physical body has given up, and we ourselves or reputable spiritual mediums can prove this. Simply put, your spirit and your consciousness can never and will never die.

Of course bereavement can be very hard for loved ones left behind, both emotionally and in terms of how their human lives change as a result. It is always a shock, even when you are fully expecting it. Thereafter, despite what others may tell you, over time you do not "get over" the loss of a true loved one in emotional terms, you can only learn to live with it and accept it.

Nevertheless your loved ones in spirit implore you to stop grieving, to get on with your remaining life and to make the most of it.

The return of the soul or spirit of the deceased – free of all bodily frailties and illnesses – to the loving welcome of past family and friends already resident in the spirit world is a blissful and indescribably positive experience. This is no fanciful assumption, it is provable fact.

And I hope that I have demonstrated the point adequately from personal insights to the readers of my narrative with open and enquiring minds.

So, having devoted the time to reading my book and possibly finding it of real interest, what have you got to lose by furthering your knowledge with a visit to an established Christian or independent spiritualist church or to a respected medium in your locality?

"Death Is Nothing At All"

In concluding I am so reminded of the poem below about the continuity of life which is often delivered at funerals. That is "Death Is Nothing At All" by Henry Scott Holland (1847-1918), Canon of St Paul's Cathedral and Regius Professor of Divinity at Oxford University.

Holland was a man keenly interested in social justice and had many outstanding spiritual qualities, insisting that the slum-dwellers of his day were owed honour precisely because they were "poor, weak and helpless". His concern for the plight of the impoverished and downtrodden working class in London mirrored that of Victor Hugo half-a-century earlier for the poor of Paris (Chapter 1).

So these famous words were included in his sermon at St Paul's in May 1910, when the body of Edward VII was lying in state at Westminster:

"Death is nothing at all.
It does not count.
I have only slipped away into the next room.
Nothing has happened.

"Everything remains exactly as it was.
I am I, and you are you,
And the old life that we lived so fondly together is untouched, unchanged.
Whatever we were to each other, that we are still.

"Call me by the old familiar name.
Speak of me in the easy way which you always used.
Put no difference into your tone.
Wear no forced air of solemnity or sorrow.

"Laugh as we always laughed at the little jokes that we enjoyed together.
Play, smile, think of me, pray for me.
Let my name be ever the household word that it always was.
Let it be spoken without an effort, without the ghost of a shadow upon it.

"Life means all that it ever meant.
It is the same as it ever was.
There is absolute and unbroken continuity.
What is this death but a negligible accident?

"Why should I be out of mind because I am out of sight?
I am but waiting for you, for an interval,
Somewhere very near,
Just around the corner.

"All is well.
Nothing is hurt; nothing is lost.
One brief moment and all will be as it was before.
How we shall laugh at the trouble of parting when we meet again!"

Henry Scott Holland www.churchtimes.co.uk

Our wedding day 25th June 1983 at Dolgellau, North Wales

Cheers! During our honeymoon, a flamenco evening at the Hotel Beverly Playa, Paguera, Majorca

Book design, layout and preparation by Marc L Pittaway, Advertising Matters Ltd, Solihull, UK

SWC

Spirit World Communications

Printed in Poland
by Amazon Fulfillment
Poland Sp. z o.o., Wrocław

10018650R20114